JOSEPHINE "SADIE" EARP
THE SORDID TRUTH
1870 – 1883

BY

PETER BRAND

Josephine "Sadie" Earp
The Sordid Truth
1870 - 1883

Peter Brand
PO Box 1030
Meadowbank, NSW 2114
Australia

ISBN: 979-8-335-22115-3

www.tombstonevendetta.com

"THE TRUTH CAN STING, BUT I WOULD RATHER BE STUNG BY THE TRUTH THAN CARESSED BY A LITANY OF LIES."

PETER BRAND

CONTENTS

Introduction   1

Acknowledgments   3

1   Secrets & Lies   5

2   The Marcus Family   11

3   San Francisco Vice   21

4   Willingly Procured   24

5   High-Class Hattie Wells   40
     & Elegant Ella Howard

6   Exit Josephine "Sadie" Marcus   55
     & Enter "Sadie Mansfield"

7   "Aunt Julia"   61

8   Prescott, Arizona Territory   64

9   Lure of the Lucre   76

10   Runaway - Yet Again   81

11   The Gambler & The Prostitute   87

      The Truth, or
      "A Nice, Clean Story"   109

      Proven Images   113

      Notes & Sources   129

      Index   143

INTRODUCTION

The author's original examination of Josephine "Sadie" Earp's early life, during the period 1870 to 1883, was first published in the *Wild West History Association* (WWHA) *Journal, March 2023*. This work was subsequently honored with the Association's Six-Shooter Award as the Best Journal Article for 2023.

This book expands on the findings published in that article. It includes additional revelations, images and information, and has now been made available to the general public in order to further shed light on the truth concerning Sadie's early years. The truth had remained elusive to most until March 2023, due to the extent to which Sadie went in order to cover up her scandalous teenage years.

Her cause was helped, in large part, due to the efforts of her previous biographers. These authors not only repeated her tall-tales, but completely ignored the primary evidence that, when thoroughly examined, made it abundantly clear that Sadie had purposely lied about her past.

In one publication, dates and places were altered to fit Sadie's false narrative, in an attempt to make her implausible story seem more palatable and believable. No thorough investigation, or analysis, was conducted into the blatant inconsistencies in her memoir by these authors. No critical investigation of any kind was done to expose her false claims of participation in a theatrical group head-lined by the famous actress, Pauline Markham, in 1879.

By doing so, these authors simply perpetuated Sadie's lies, and made it harder for genuine historians and discerning readers to sort the fact from the fiction. Photographs, with no provenance, claiming to be "Sadie" were also included in these publications, and only served to further muddy the waters.

This book corrects those misrepresentations, and explores the impoverished environment in which Josephine "Sadie" Earp (nee Marcus) lived as a young girl. Her rebellious behavior and her character are fully investigated, and the reader is informed about the influence of the San Francisco vice trade, and how it impacted her choices and catered to her need for excitement. New primary sourced evidence exposes the truth about Sadie's early life and adds necessary depth to the story of the Marcus family. The book takes a forensic "deep-dive" approach as to dates, places, people and important wording and commentary in Sadie's own memoir.

It is also important to note that only verified photographs of Josephine "Sadie" Earp were used in this book. There are no verified images available of her in her younger years, as at the date of publication.

ACKNOWLEDGMENTS

I would like to pay my respects to the late Carol Mitchell, and the late Roger Jay, for their ground-breaking research into the early life of Josephine "Sadie" Earp (nee Marcus). Credit is also due to Sherry Monahan for her thorough research of the Marcus family's early years in San Francisco.

Many thanks are due to Mike Mihaljevich for his assistance with the cover-art for this publication, and for his friendship and encouragement. Thanks also to Mike Mayberry, Donna Dycus, Jean Smith, David Guyton and Anastasia Sitnina for their help, support, kindness and willingness to promote my work. Brad Courtney and Lesley Jenkinson have also generously assisted with their time and insightful observations.

Special thanks are also due to Roy Young, and the Wild West History Association (WWHA), for publishing the latest research, by independent authors and researchers, in their quarterly WWHA *Journal*.

"THE TRUTH IS RARELY PURE,
AND NEVER SIMPLE."

OSCAR WILDE

1
SECRETS & LIES

When Josephine "Sadie" Earp (nee Marcus) decided it was time to tell the story of her life in 1937, she had a big problem. Her early life and that of her family was far from ideal, and the way she dealt with such potential embarrassments was to simply wipe them from her story, or invent a more acceptable fictional story to compensate. She had previously tried this method, with some success, in regards to the biography of her common-law husband and life-long partner, Wyatt Earp, written by Stuart Lake and published in 1931.

Josephine was a strong-willed and determined woman who managed to have her own name and that of Wyatt's "wife," former prostitute Mattie Blaylock, kept out of Lake's book. This was no small feat, since both women were present in Tombstone at the same time, and both had much in common. The fact that Blaylock ended up committing suicide, accidentally or otherwise, after Wyatt had deserted her in favor of the younger and more appealing Josephine, would not have reflected well. Having erased both herself and Blaylock from the pages of Earp's story, she then tried to use similar tactics, and more, in relation to dictating her own memoir. 1

Josephine, or "Josie," as she preferred to be known after Wyatt's death, was in her mid-seventies in 1937 and was not faring too well – financially and emotionally – after the death, in 1936, of her wealthy sister, Henrietta, aka "Hattie." Josie was then cut off by Henrietta's children and, as a result, decided to reach out to Wyatt's relatives, sisters Mabel Earp Cason and Vinnolia Earp Ackerman, for help to write her memoir.

Mabel and Vinnolia agreed, and allowed Josie to live at their homes while they worked on the project. What followed was a torturous four-year effort to pry factual information from Josie about her early years, her time in Tombstone, and exactly how and when she met and began her love affair with Wyatt Earp. It proved to be an impossible task. The sisters eventually gave up on the project, as Josie refused to provide accurate chronological details of all the factual information that would be required to form a publishable book. 2

Josie was determined to paint herself as a nice, stage-struck, fun-loving girl, who came from a wealthy German family. In order to do so, she employed her previous tactic of leaving out crucial information if it was considered potentially embarrassing; completely ignoring certain people, places and events for similar reasons and, worse still, changing names, inventing false scenarios and continually lying about her early years. The manuscript remained a chronological mess. It was a curious collection of disjointed memories, with large time-gaps and untruthful, or missing, information about Josie's formative years from 1870 to 1883. It also left a veritable chasm in regards to the facts about Tombstone, and how and when she actually met Wyatt Earp, and later became his partner.

When Vinnolia Earp Ackerman passed away, in 1954, Mabel Earp Cason kept their many typed stories and the notes they had taken, as well as their attempted drafts. These eventually became known as the "Cason Manuscript." While the unedited version of the manuscript remained unpublished, a version was printed and made available for public perusal by historian Earl Chafin, in the mid-1990s. 3

In creating her "story," Josie avoided some very unpleasant truths, though the information that was included inadvertently guided diligent researchers, if they were willing to dig hard enough. The late historian Carol Mitchell was the first of these writer/researchers to "join the dots," when she published her theory that Josie was actually the prostitute, Sadie Mansfield, in her article "Lady Sadie" for *True West* in 2001. The article raised eyebrows, but did not seal the deal. 4

In 2013, the late historian Roger Jay, a diligent and extremely articulate writer/researcher, went even further in his ground-breaking article for the Wild West

Josephine "Sadie" Earp, circa 1921.
(Courtesy *True West* Magazine)

History Association *Journal*, entitled *"Face to Face: Sadie Mansfield/Josephine Sarah Marcus."* Jay's in-depth research presented Mitchell's theory, but with an incredibly accurate critical analysis of the Cason Manuscript. Jay held Josie to account in terms of the dates, places, events, and the people included in her flawed memoir. He completely demolished any possibility that Josie had been truthful about why, when and with whom she had originally traveled to Tombstone. In doing so, he added considerable weight to Mitchell's original theory.

In the interests of full disclosure, it is important to acknowledge that I worked as a researcher for Jay in gathering some, but certainly not all, of the information he used in that article. Once again, his article created interest in Josie's early life, as it was fast becoming obvious, even to the uninitiated, that something was radically wrong with Josie's version of events as to her arrival in Arizona, not just once, but twice. 5

Much to her credit, author Sherry Monahan clearly summarized Jay's findings, and then produced even more of her own in her excellent book, *Mrs. Earp: The Wives and Lovers of the Earp Brothers*. Monahan was of the same opinion in regards to Josie's suspect story-telling, stating "She [Josie] always made sure no one knew the true story of what happened while she was in Arizona… forever taking her secrets to the grave, just as she wanted." 6

Sometimes, as Roger Jay pointed out, it was not only what was stated in the Cason Manuscript that caused considerable doubt about Josie's tall-tales, but also pertinent information and important names that Josie refused to mention, that prompted speculation about her story. The fact that Josie chose to lie so blatantly, just fuelled the fire of researchers like Mitchell and Jay and prompted more questions from Monahan.

Josie had good reasons to avoid the truth, because the truth, in her case, was often sordid, sometimes confronting, and certainly not the way an elderly woman, or some of her family, would want to be remembered.

To fully understand Josie's early years, it is necessary to thoroughly trawl through the seedy reports of San Francisco's vile underbelly. Newspapers carried detailed descriptions of the people who peddled vice in the city. These reports revealed the temptations and living conditions of the poor and displaced immigrants who called the city their home in the 1870s.

San Francisco was a teeming metropolis with distinct districts separating, among other things, the privileged from the poor, and, despite her untruthful claims to the contrary, Josephine's father was not a successful merchant; her family was actually quite poor and deemed to be from the lower working class within the Jewish community. 7

2

THE MARCUS FAMILY

Josephine's father Hyman, or Henry, Marcus was a Jewish baker who, according to census records, was born in Prussia, in 1836. He immigrated to New York, where he met and married Sophia Lewis, who was six years his senior. Although she was probably also a Prussian Jew, her background is far from clear. She had a daughter, presumably from a previous marriage, named Rebecca, who was born in Missouri in 1851, or 1852. Sophia then produced three more children with Hyman Marcus, all born in New York – Nathan in 1857, Josephine "Sadie" in late 1860, or early 1861, and Henrietta "Hattie" in 1863. 8

The Marcus family made the bold move from New York to San Francisco by early 1870, where Sophia's first daughter, then known as Rebecca Levy, married another Prussian Jew, named Aaron Wiener, on April 30, 1870. Rebecca seemed to have chosen wisely, as Wiener was a 29-year-old clothing merchant who lived with his father, Isaac. Together, father and son worked in the family retail clothing business, with Aaron listing his personal asset worth, around the time of his marriage to Rebecca, as $1,200. 9

Hyman Marcus and his family were first listed in San Francisco in the 1870 federal census enumeration as living at 1211 Powell Street, tantalizingly close to the exotic, and enticing, Chinatown district. The previous year, the same premises had been advertised as housing William Spader's Saloon and Billiard Room, so it can only be imagined how suitable the locality was for a family home.

Hyman worked as a baker for the Overland Bakery, conveniently located on the same street, and stated his personal assets were valued at only $100. In what was to become a recurring theme for the Marcus family, the spelling of their name in official records changed almost as often as their address. In the 1870 San Francisco census, for example, Hyman was listed at the Powell Street address as "Henry Maroux." 10

Josephine and her sister, Henrietta, attended the local Powell Street Primary School and, in her memoir, she recalled this place as not being to her liking. She clashed with the school principal, "Miss Benjamin," over attendance issues. This information in her memoir seems to be accurate, as Carrie Benjamin was the principal of the school at that time. Exactly how often Josephine attended school is a matter for debate as, by her own admission, she thought the treatment she received there was harsh and draconian, in contrast to the bold and bohemian sights and sounds of the streets of nearby Chinatown. 11

12

Chinatown certainly held a fascination for Josephine, and she vividly described the busy and overpopulated district, admitting that her "childish mind" was occupied with the exotic sights, sounds and scents of the region. She also mentioned playing jacks with her younger sister on the doorstep of their house, which indicated the time period she was describing was probably late 1870; a time when the family lived near Chinatown and she was only nine or ten years-old. 12

Her memories of these times sound quite carefree, but the question has to be asked how her father was able to afford rent, food, clothing and household-goods for himself, his wife and their three children, as well as their education, on a humble baker's wage? The answer was that he probably could not. Times must have been very tough, although Josephine could not mention the true state of affairs as she had claimed the family was comfortable and prosperous.

One major omission from her memoir was her older brother, Nathan Marcus. She failed to make any mention of him in her entire manuscript. In this case, his omission may have been intentional in order to avoid embarrassment for the family. It seems that Nathan, at the age of thirteen, had left home and was living on the street, estranged from his family. On October 18, 1870 a thirteen-year-old boy, reported as "Marcus Nathan," (sic) was arraigned in the police court for breaking the windows of a Chinese wash-house. Nathan gave evidence that he did not live with his parents and, therefore, had his washing done at the laundry, but had no money to pay for the services. The Chinese had refused to return his bundle without payment, so he decided to break their shop windows in retaliation. After hearing all the facts of the case, a police court judge committed Nathan to an indefinite term at the San Francisco Industrial School for boys. 13

INDUSTRIAL SCHOOL.

San Francisco Industrial School for Boys, circa 1871.
(Courtesy California Historical Society)

When arrested, Nathan may have tried to reverse his first and last name in order to give an alias, or the newspaper reporters may simply have made a transcription mistake. Whatever the case, the boy spent at least the next year at the institution, which was notorious for its lack of financing, poor facilities and the very basic nature of the education available for its inmates. It was located a good distance from the city, so this would have made visitations difficult for Sophia and Hyman, aka Henry. Just over one year later, the minutes of the institution's monthly Board of Managers meeting were published in the *San Francisco Chronicle*. The report noted that "a communication was read from the mother of a boy named Nathan Marcus, asking for his discharge." The matter was then referred to the Visiting Committee for their consideration. The result of her plea was not published. 14

By the time Sophia Marcus had written to the Industrial School, her family's situation had not improved. This would not have helped her plea for Nathan's release, as they had moved to an even poorer section of the city. Listed in the 1871 city directory as "Hyman Marcuse," the baker and his family then resided at 550 Clara Street. Their new neighborhood was known to be "south of the Slot." The "Slot" was the center of Market Street; north of the Slot were the theaters, hotels and shopping districts, while to the south were the factories, slums, laundries, machine shops, boiler-works and the small dwellings of the poorer working class. 15

The San Francisco city directories are a good guide to the reality of Josephine's disjointed life during the period 1870 to 1873. There was no stability in terms of home location, and this could have contributed to her already restless nature. Her father, the sole earner in the family, was unable to rise above his humble status and, in 1872, the records show he was listed as "Henry Marcuse" at 109 Shipley Street, just around the corner from their previous dwelling. Henry was listed as a "Peddler" – probably of baked goods.

Although she disliked traditional school, Josephine claimed that, around this time, she and her younger sister, Henrietta, were able to attend dance classes at nearby Howard Street.

McCarty Dance Academy, Dashaway Hall, San Francisco
(Courtesy sanfranciscotheatres.blogspot.com)

According to her memoir, the two girls were taught at the McCarthy (sic) Academy of Dancing, which was actually operated by the McCarty brothers and sisters, at the Dashaway Hall on Post Street. 16

If Josephine was being truthful in regard to those dance classes, she and Henrietta had a long walk, up 4th Street to reach the academy, as there was no record of a dance school on Howard Street. She also claimed to have been given music lessons by a "Mrs Hirsch," who just happened to be the mother of her best friend, whom she referred to as "Dora Hirsch." In reality, it may have been Josephine's older half-sister, Rebecca Wiener, who paid for her dancing and music lessons, if they did actually occur, as it is hard to imagine how her own father could have afforded such extravagances.

Thanks to the research of Roger Jay, however, we now know that Dora and Mrs. Hirsch did not exist – at least not under those names. Jay's research showed that the likely inspirations for these two characters were Betsy Hirschberg, a music teacher, and her talented daughter, Leah Hirschberg, who lived a couple of blocks away on 3rd Street. Betsy's husband, Meyer, operated a bakery, and may have known Henry Marcus in the course of their work. Leah was a year younger than Josephine, but the two girls may well have been schoolmates during the period 1872 to 1873. 17

Josephine also claimed that her half-sister, Rebecca, would take her and Henrietta to the theater, and that her love of watching stage performances was due to the generosity of Rebecca. As she recalled, "my eldest sister was a constant theater-goer and every Saturday afternoon for years, she took either Hattie or me to a matinee." It is highly unusual, therefore, that in the unedited Cason Manuscript, Josephine failed to state her half-sister's married surname, [Wiener] and inexplicably only referred to her as "Edna." The reason for this attempted deception, again, may have been to hide family secrets related to her brother-in-law, which would come to light in future years. 18

Ironically, it may have been those visits to the theater district that brought Josephine into the full view of the gamblers and prostitutes who frequented the Saturday matinees. The high-class working girls often partnered with San Francisco's gamblers, known as "sporting men," and, together or separately, these members of the city's underbelly gathered in the theater district on Saturdays at matinee time. They dressed to impress and sauntered in and out of shows, with the women openly displaying fine dresses, with glittering jewelry and accessories.

In her memoir, Josephine specifically mentioned the thrill she felt, as a young girl, seeing "the elegant gowns of the women in the dress circle." She had probably just witnessed the flashy gamblers and colorful high-class prostitutes, dressed to entice. In any case, she did admit to having a fascination with the entire atmosphere of the matinees, and those who attended and performed. 19

In keeping with their previous habit of annually moving house, the 1873 San Francisco City Directory found the Marcus family back at Clara Street, but this time located at No. 221. Henry was still listed as a baker, but with one very noticeable change – his name was recorded as "Henry Marks." Future events would indicate this more anglicized version of the "Marcus" name appeared to have been intentional, rather than a misspelling. 20

Josephine spoke fondly in the memoir of this period of her life, and specifically mentioned playing with the children of two families, named Fromberg and Belasco, who also lived on Clara Street. Although she failed to include exact dates, she did inadvertently provide the time-period in this case, as the only time the Fromberg and Belasco families lived "a few doors up" from Josephine at 221 Clara Street was during the years 1873 and 1874. 21

Although her memories of these years sounded carefree and whimsical, Josephine, by her own admission, had developed a tendency to act impulsively and against the will of her parents. This behavior manifested itself in truancy, having her ears pierced, encouraging her younger sister, Hattie, to disobey her parents, and a general ambition to, one day, be part of the fancy matinee crowd that she so admired.

As stated bluntly in her memoir, "such was the life in which Josephine Sarah Marcus grew up and, as might be expected, she matured early, for there was far too much excitement in the air for one to remain a child." 22

This comment hinted at future activities that both Mabel Earp Cason and Vinnolia Earp Ackerman could not have imagined when they recorded this veiled admission by Sadie.

California Theater, Bush Street,
San Francisco, circa 1870.
(Courtesy Mike Mihaljevich)

3

SAN FRANCISCO VICE

At this time, San Francisco, like all major cities, endured the presence of a thriving vice trade. Whether it was brothels, gambling houses, opium dens, or rough saloons, the city's vice purveyors catered for every ethnicity, and every class of person. The region of the city known as the "The Barbary Coast" was the most dangerous and debauched area in San Francisco. It was said to be roughly bordered by Broadway, Stockton, Clay and Montgomery Streets, including part of Chinatown, and was a "no-go" zone after dark for most decent people. The region was close to the notorious Waverly Place, which was populated with many, but certainly not all, of the brothels in the city. 23

The 1870 federal census revealed that both young and mature women, from all over the world, worked as prostitutes and madams within dwellings on Waverly Place and Sacramento Street. These bagnios ranged from overcrowded basic crib rooms, to lavishly appointed high-class establishments. 24

Sadly, many of the women who worked in the lower-class brothels suffered from disease, neglect, drug and alcohol addiction, as well as violence and abuse. Suicide was not uncommon and new girls were always being recruited, as the turn-over rate was high. Some girls died, some were procured for other towns, while a few accepted offers from gamblers to become their common-law wives. This often simply meant that their "husband" acted as their pimp, in order to help entice suckers to their gambling dens.

In July, 1873, the *San Francisco Chronicle* expressed disgust at the number of very young girls who were being enticed into prostitution; their headline read, "Ruined Lives - Alarming Increase of Immorality Among Young Girls in the City."

Their article included information from recent police court hearings, where girls from the tender ages of ten to sixteen had been targeted by unscrupulous men and women. One report noted that four schoolgirls had been procured, and then relocated to brothels in Sacramento and San Jose. Another newspaper noted that a very young girl had been taken in San Francisco, by a well-known prostitute, for transport to Pioche, a notoriously wild silver camp in Nevada.

While some girls from wealthy backgrounds found their way to Waverley Place and other brothels, the largest number were orphaned, or from broken, violent, or poor immigrant homes. Various methods were used to trawl the city for female children and, for the procurers, any method was acceptable. Typically, these vile women and men would frequent areas around the poorer school districts, disreputable dance schools, theater matinees, and public squares, waiting and watching for potential marks. If the recruitment was successful, some girls were taken straight to the brothels, while others might be sold to a third party and removed to other towns. 25

There was a sinister presence in and around the area in which Josephine lived that she, understandably, failed to mention in her memoir. The threat to young girls in San Francisco was very real, particularly south of the Slot.

Prostitutes of various ages pose for a photograph in an 1890 San Francisco brothel.
(Courtesy San Francisco History Center)

4

WILLINGLY PROCURED

While Josephine seemed happy to mention a few playmates in her memoir, such as the Fromberg and Belasco children and "Dora Hirsch" (actually Leah Hirschberg), she failed to mention anyone else. As usual, she had very good reasons to ignore and omit the names of other more rebellious children, with whom she had adventures, such as the McCloud sisters and the Cassidy sisters – girls of Scottish and Irish heritage from her local neighborhood. These girls were not playing jacks and dancing around the maypole, but had a much harder edge, with reckless attitudes to match. Josephine, despite her unconvincing claims to the contrary, was similarly reckless and, like her brother Nathan, possessed a deep desire to break away from the constraints of her impoverished family life.

The McCloud sisters lived around the corner from Josephine, on Shipley Street, and were the daughters of a Scottish bartender. Katy Cassidy lived with her wayward sister, Mary, and their Irish parents, Bridget and John, nearby on Everett Street, where her father worked as a wagon driver. An example of the environment in which the Cassidy sisters were raised

24

was reflected in a police report that noted both Bridget and John Cassidy had been arrested, and charged with the use of vulgar language in March, 1872. The couple were subsequently found to be guilty in the police court, and fined $5 each. 26

Sometime prior to September, 1873, a notorious prostitute and procurer, known as Emma Hopper, began operations south of the Slot. Once described by a reporter as one of "worst women to have ever lived," Hopper then came into contact with Josephine, aged only twelve, Katy Cassidy and the McCloud sisters. Josephine was said to be a dark-haired pretty girl, who was shapely beyond her years – exactly the type of girl who was targeted by procurers.

Hopper based her operations in a boarding house on the corner of 3rd and Stevenson streets, and then at 17 4th Street, both just below the Slot. They were central locations from which she could easily travel down 3rd or 4th streets to the poorer dwellings, and then lure girls back to her lodgings for eventual transfer into Chinatown, the Waverly Place brothels, or beyond. 27

Exact details of how Josephine and Emma Hopper became acquainted, and when her grooming started, are lacking. Hopper's reputation was not only well known among the demimonde, but was also whispered within the upper class, as she sometimes fulfilled requests from wealthy men for girls with specific attributes, and of certain ages and appearance.

Hopper was also known to the three other girls – Lizzie McCloud aged fourteen, her sister, Annie McCloud aged twelve, and Katy Cassidy aged fourteen. 28

On Sunday morning, September 7, 1873 Josephine, Katy Cassidy and the McCloud sisters left their various homes and met with an associate of Hopper's, a prostitute who gave her name as Nancy "Nellie" Reese. The four girls then walked, or were willingly transported by Reese, to a brothel on Geary Street, east of Dupont, [now known as Grant Avenue] north of the Slot. Josephine and her companions were fed, and presumably told of a future that would include fine dresses, good money and a better, more exciting life. They then spent Sunday night sleeping at the Geary Street brothel.

The following day, they were instructed to relocate to the Broadway Boarding House, on the corner of Broadway and Kearny, which may have indicated they were to be sold to a third-party. The four girls did so, and Nellie Reese paid $4 to rent a room on the second floor, and gave the runaways $1 to go and buy something to eat.

The reports of these events made it clear that the girls were not kidnapped, and were free to go and buy food, confirming they were not under any form of restraint at the Broadway Boarding House. They could have returned to their homes on Sunday or Monday, but Josephine and her friends chose not to do so. 29

Dupont Street, San Francisco, near Chinatown.
(Courtesy California State Library)

On Sunday evening, the parents of the girls waited in vain for their return. Monday morning, being a work day, meant that their respective fathers arose and went to their jobs, while their worried mothers, Sophia Marcus (aka Marks), Anna McCloud and Bridget Cassidy all went to the city hall police station to report that their girls were missing. A search was conducted by the police throughout Monday, without any success. As night fell, so must the hopes of Josephine's family. 30

On Monday evening, Mrs. Moore, who ran the Broadway Boarding House with her husband, reported to the city hall police station and stated she had observed several young girls in one of her rooms with Nellie Reese. She gave descriptions of the girls that seemed to match the missing runaways, so police detectives John Coffey and Edward Devitt, who specialized in rescuing girls from procurers, rushed to the scene. Between 9 and 10 o'clock on Monday night, they raided the place and found the four missing girls and Nellie Reese in a second-story room. All were taken into custody and transported to city hall, where they were immediately sent to the chief of police's office for questioning. 31

San Francisco Detective, John Coffey.
(*San Francisco Morning Call*, January 18, 1893)

Police reporters from both the *San Francisco Chronicle* and the *San Francisco Morning Call* were on hand to cover the case, and both specifically commented on the defiant and contemptuous attitude displayed by all four girls.

The *Chronicle* had a policy of not revealing the names of underage girls in these scenarios, in order to spare their families from what they knew would be extreme embarrassment. Their reporter observed that all the girls were "unabashed at their arrest," and the only thing most of them feared was meeting their mothers again. One girl, in particular, had no such qualms, and "plainly showed she had neither fear, nor respect, for her mother, and only displayed emotion of any kind when told that she would spend the night in the San Francisco County Jail." 32

The *Morning Call* did not share the same compassionate attitude as their competitor, and not only provided the offenders names, but also included their addresses – "Annie and Lizzie McCloud of No. 66 Shipley Street; Katy Cassidy of No. 25 Everett Street, and Josephine Marks [Marcus] of No. 221 Clara Street." The *Morning Call* reporter also felt compelled to mention the girls' attitudes and stated that they "astonished" observers "with their boldness and the manner in which they demeaned themselves." 33

Bridget Cassidy was the first mother to arrive at city hall that night, and immediately asked her daughter

29

where she had been. Katy Cassidy sarcastically told her to "go and find out," and then sharply barked at her mother to "Hush up, and don't bother me with your talk." In frustration, Bridget Cassidy then turned to another of the girls and said, among other things, "I think you are a bad girl." The girl in question snapped back, "You talk about a bad girl, you had better look at your own daughter – she is as bad as I am, if not worse." This response could have come from Josephine, but was more likely to have been said by the older girl, Lizzie McCloud. 34

At 10:30 p.m., Nellie Reese, who denied charges that she "was training the girls for a life of shame," was lodged in the city jail. Defiant Josephine and her three bold companions were taken to the county jail and handed over to the matron at that facility, who locked them in the cells for the night. All of them, including Nellie Reese, were to face a judge at the police court the next day. 35

On Tuesday morning, September 9, Josephine and the other three girls were transported back from the county jail. They then stood in the police court before Judge Davis Louderback, the 32-year-old former city prosecutor, who was to hear the evidence and decide their immediate futures.

The families, no doubt, were very concerned that Judge Louderback would send their daughters to the Magdalen Asylum, as he had already sent thirteen girls, of similar ages, to the Asylum in just the past three months. The "Mag," as it was commonly known at the time, was run by Catholic nuns, the Sisters of Mercy, who had come from Ireland. The main purpose of the institution was to rehabilitate young girls and women who had appeared before the courts in relation to prostitution, but it also accepted recalcitrant girls who had fallen on hard times and committed offenses such as thieving and vagrancy.

Some girls were even voluntarily committed to the "Mag" by poor, or frustrated, parents who could not prevent their daughters from associating with thugs, prostitutes, and pimps. The 1880 federal census showed the Asylum housed girls as young as twelve and women as old as sixty. Named in honor of the redeemed biblical prostitute, Mary Magdalene, the institution had a reputation for rigid rules and hard work. Girls were taught sewing and seamstress skills, the products of which were then sold to help finance the ongoing operation of the Asylum.

It is clear, from newspaper reports of their behavior, that all the girls were fully aware of the Magdalen Asylum and the consequences of their actions. This was evident after their arrest, because Josephine and her friends openly expressed their dread of being sent to the "Mag." Newspaper reporters noted the girls feared the Asylum, but steeled each other with the resolve that they would all face it together. 36

Davis Louderback.

Police Court Judge, Davis Louderback, had previously
been the San Francisco City Police Prosecutor.
(*San Francisco Examiner*, January 21, 1902)

After hearing the evidence, Judge Louderback, who was probably influenced by the fact that all three mothers had quickly reported their children missing and obviously cared for their welfare, ruled that the runaway girls should be returned to their homes.

Louderback then turned his attention and gavel to young prostitute, Nellie Reese. Weighing up all the evidence, he dismissed the charges against her, as it could not be proved that the girls were taken against their will. She walked free, but then simply returned to the streets and continued her life of prostitution, drug use and general degradation, possibly under the alias of "Nellie Schwartz," who had been known to work with Emma Hopper that same year. 37

Henry and Sophia Marcus must have breathed a combined sigh of relief, but they then knew exactly what Josephine was capable of, and that must have been cause for constant concern. The fact that not only Josephine's name, but the family's full address, had been released to the general public by the *Morning Call* also, no doubt, caused them much shame. 38

When reporting on the release of the four girls, the *Chronicle* took the opportunity to castigate the *Morning Call* under the headline – "Indignation at the Wanton Exposure of their Names and Residences." The *Chronicle* defended its own policy of withholding names and readily explained why – "The parents of the children were deeply mortified by the course of the

Morning Call in publishing the names and residences, and very thankful to the *Chronicle* for withholding them. They said they could not see any public good was gained by thus blasting the reputations of their children and making them objects of perpetual scorn among their playmates. They regard this action of the *Call* as placing the most difficult obstacles in the way, which they will have to contend with in turning their daughter's footsteps into virtuous paths." The *Chronicle* finished off by emphasizing that releasing their names and addresses was "often the means of forever closing the door for a reformation." [39]

Eventually, this proved to be a profound statement in regards to Elizabeth "Lizzie" McCloud, Catherine "Katy" Cassidy and Josephine "Sadie" Marcus, as none could resist the high-risk life of a prostitute.

Lizzie McCloud ended up in the Magdalen Asylum in 1877, for further indiscretions when aged seventeen, and spent at least three years incarcerated there. She was probably the prostitute of the same name who, after a life of shame, committed suicide in Stockton in 1895, by way of a morphine overdose. [40]

Katy Cassidy's fate was even worse. Her older sister, Mary, was committed to the Magdalen Asylum in March 1875, having "fallen into disreputable ways and become the associate of hoodlums." Mary's behavior led Katy further into the murky underbelly, south of the Slot. In February, 1877 Katy Cassidy was arrested and charged with "battery." While being transported to her bail hearing, Katy seduced the police officer entrusted with her security. The pair failed to appear in court, but rather spent the night together. Katy Cassidy was eventually locked up, and the police officer was dismissed from the force. [41]

Upon her release from the Magdalen Asylum, Mary Cassidy took up with a thug named John Martin and moved into a shanty on Converse Street, in an unsavory region of San Francisco known as "Tar Flat." Katy Cassidy eventually moved in with her sister, Mary, and then partnered with two brothers, named Andrew and Thomas Cain, who acted as her pimps. Their shanty was known as a "disorderly house," and "the headquarters of hoodlums who held nightly orgies," from where Mary Cassidy "distributed circulars inducing immoral behavior." [42]

Both Katy and Mary Cassidy, now fully committed to a life of degradation and crime, suffered violence, spent time in the House of Corrections and became addicted to alcohol. This lifestyle predictably resulted in the premature death of Mary on October 11, 1881, while her sister, Katy Cassidy, died shortly after on January 2, 1882, aged only 22. [43]

The obvious dangers of the sex trade, likewise, did not deter young Josephine Marcus. She had become a risk-taker at the tender age of twelve, and this then became her way of life. Despite the publication of their address, however, her family continued to reside at 221 Clara Street during 1874. This was the first time in the previous four years that the family had managed to remain at the same address in consecutive years.

The reason may have been that the family now had a second income. Josephine's wayward brother, Nathan, had been released from the Industrial School by 1873, as "Nathan Markus" (sic) was arrested for a misdemeanour and fined $5 by the Police Court on December 16, 1873. He was then listed in the 1874 San Francisco City Directory as "Nathan Marks," a trunk maker for Herman Behrendt & Co., who resided at 221 Clara Street. One of the ways that an inmate could be offered a release from the Industrial School was to be indentured to an employer, and this may have been the case for Nathan, as he was aged only seventeen in 1874. His father was listed in the same directory as "Henry Marks," a baker, at the 221 Clara Street address. 44

The fact that the family was able to remain at 221 Clara Street, and Nathan had returned to the fold, were positive signs, but Josephine and her family may well have been suffering from the stigma attached to her arrest, as predicted by the *Chronicle*.

Josephine admitted in her memoir that she had not been fond of school, and her reputation as a defiant runaway would-be prostitute, with a contemptuous attitude toward authority, would not have endeared her to the school administrators, or some of her classmates, and certainly not their parents. An advertisement placed in a newspaper, six months after her arrest, strongly suggested that Josephine was actually no longer attending school. The newspaper editions dated March 26 & 27, 1874 included an advertisement which read as follows – "Situation Wanted – By A Competent girl to do general housework in a small family, Call at 221 Clara." (See below) 45

SITUATION WANTED—BY A COM-
petent girl, to do general housework in a
small family. Call at 221 Clara street. m26 3t°

This work request, in all likelihood, related to Josephine, as the only other known girl at the address was her sister Henrietta, aged only ten or eleven, and it was inconceivable that Henrietta would have been forced out of school and into work.

The term "Situation" was used, in most cases, to mean that the girl would move in with the family for whom she worked. This form of steady work may have been seen as the best way to ease the financial struggle of her family, and for Josephine to learn discipline, and the value of earning a small wage.

It also implied that the best place for Josephine, at this stage, was not in her own family home. In fact, given her bold and "contemptuous attitude" after her previous arrest, Sophia and Henry Marcus may have been concerned that Josephine would lead her younger sister, Henrietta, down the same path. That scenario had unfolded with Lizzie McCloud and her younger sister, Annie, as well as with Mary and Katy Cassidy.

Unfortunately, sometimes procurers used these advertisements to find potential prey. A smartly attired woman would call at the premises and assess the girl's appearance and situation. If the procurer liked what she saw, fraudulent references and details of the home where the work was to be performed would be provided, and better than basic pay would be offered. Some poorer families often then allowed their daughters to leave with the procurer.

ORPHAN—WANTED A YOUNG GIRL from 11 to 14 years of age to be company and take charge of a child; to go in the country. Apply at 722 Filbert street.   m25-3t*

"Orphan – Wanted A Young Girl from 11 to 14 years of age to be company and take charge of a child; to go in the country. Appy at 722 Filbert Street."

Suspicious advertisements, like the one above, published in the *San Francisco Chronicle* May 26, 1873, were often brazenly used by procurers to recruit girls into a life of prostitution.

The San Francisco Police Department had examples where the procurer would return to the family home and pay a monthly wage to the girl's parents, who would be informed that all was well. In other cases, the police knew of daughters, having been seduced into a luxurious brothel life-style, who would still visit their parents occasionally, and lie as to their real occupation, to allay any further investigation. 46

The situation was so dire during the period 1870 to 1875, that two police officers were dedicated to investigating and rescuing under-age girls from procurers and brothels. The police were understaffed and overworked and many girls disappeared as a result.

Not surprisingly, it is at this stage of Josephine's memoir, as author Roger Jay correctly noted, that her childhood comes to an abrupt end. The memoir only contains random comments regarding well known events from San Francisco's history and, between 1874 and 1879, the only person that Josephine mentioned, apart from her family, was her so-called best friend, Dora Hirsch (actually Leah Hirschberg).

The reason for the lack of personal detail related directly to her need to cover up most of her teenage past. It was a past that would take another sordid turn, and would be heavily influenced not by her schoolgirl best friend, as she stated, but by two women whose names would not look good in anyone's memoir – Hattie Wells and Ella Howard. 47

5

HIGH-CLASS HATTIE WELLS

&

ELEGANT ELLA HOWARD

Hattie A. Wells claimed a New York heritage, but she was schooled in the houses of ill-fame and saloons on the tough streets of San Francisco's Barbary Coast during the 1860s. California census records dated June 12, 1860 show she was living next door to 823 Clay Street, near the corner of Waverly Place, with several very wealthy prostitutes, all aged in their twenties. In 1860, Hattie gave her age as 28, and claimed her own personal worth was a healthy $1,500. The fact that Wells shared the premises with three other wealthy women, and they employed a full-time house keeper, indicated their establishment probably catered to a higher class of clientele. 48

It is interesting to note that their neighbor, another wealthy high-class prostitute, named Susan Morgan, was indicted several times for prostitution and keeping a house of ill-fame in the 1860s. Yet, there were no such reports for Hattie Wells, or any of the women with whom she was living and working. This fact implies that the brothel where Wells operated was paying bribes to the police to be left unmolested, while Susan Morgan was not. 49

Wells graduated up through the ranks from being a prostitute in 1860, to being the madam of her own brothel business, disguised as a bar, in 1862. The San Francisco tax records for 1862 and 1863 show Hattie A. Wells was running an establishment at nearby 722 Commercial Street, in partnership with another prostitute named Julia Summers. 50

During the 1860s, Wells evolved into a savvy business-woman and accumulated considerable funds from her bar and brothel business. In 1868, she decided to bring a new group of prostitutes to San Francisco from New York. She booked passage on the steamship *Montana*, with another madam named Lizzie Devoe, and the two set sail from San Francisco to Panama City on August 14, 1868. The pair then rode by rail to Aspinwall on the Isthmus of Panama, and sailed on the steamship *Ocean Queen* for New York City. They successfully concluded their trip, without incident, on September 5, 1868. This was an expensive exercise and again highlighted Wells' wealth, as one-way trips, including Fist-Class cabins and transfers, were valued at $100 per person. 51

Hattie Wells then spent the next three weeks in New York City recruiting six of the best girls available.

Having completed the task, Wells then booked passage, and the group commenced the return trip, sailing out of New York City, aboard the steamship *Rising Star* on October 1, 1868, bound for Aspinwall.

The women were all white, but of various ages, and included a friend from Hattie Wells' youth named Florence Adams, a beautiful 18-year-old blonde named Maud Duval, a young girl from England who went by the alias "Minnie Bell," while Mollie Pennington, Emma Seymour and Kate Arnold completed the bevy. All were listed on the ship's manifest, which meant the women occupied First-Class cabins. Less fortunate passengers were housed in the steerage section of the ship and were not named. A detachment of US troops also made the trip, and may have provided the girls with some steady income during the journey. 52

The *Rising Star* arrived safely in Aspinwall on October 14, 1868 and the conspicuous group of attractive women then traveled to Panama City. There, Wells secured passage to San Francisco on the steamship, *Golden Age*, which then sailed north. The only incident of note occurred half way through the voyage when a steerage passenger fell overboard and drowned. Hattie and her six recruits, however, arrived safely in San Francisco on October 25, 1868. 53

Wells and her ladies then went to work in a large, lavish 23-room, three-story, building located at No. 3 Waverly Place, near the intersection of Sacramento

Street. This area housed several large "houses of white prostitution," but Hattie's place was not your usual brothel. The *San Francisco Chronicle* reporters who visited the Wells "palace" in December, 1869 described it as having very expensive furnishings and carpets, beautiful wall hangings, chandeliers, and luxurious fittings seen only in the houses of the very wealthy. Several "handsomely costumed" women played cards in an adjoining waiting room, while a German pianist played classical music on an expensive Chickering square piano. Beautiful women glided through the waiting rooms and each had their own private elegant bedroom, separate from the client rooms, which were also lavishly appointed.

Wells was on-hand to greet any new arrivals, and it was noted that some of her girls were well educated, and engaged in conversations ranging from politics to

Hattie Wells owned a Chickering square piano, as above. This was typical of the expensive furniture at her brothel.

Waverly Place, San Francisco, circa 1870s.
(Courtesy California State Library)

music and the arts. Hattie's clientele were generally wealthy, and the price for their entertainment matched their status. 54

As seedy as the actual business was, Hattie Wells treated her employees and customers in the best possible way, and gained a reputation with the upper-class in San Francisco. Apart from her working girls, in 1869, Wells also employed a mulatto house-keeper and cook known as "Aunt Bess," and a mulatto porter who may have provided security for the women.

Two of her most popular working girls were Minnie Bell and Maud Duval. Both had attracted a lot of attention when attending the Saturday theater matinees by dressing in the most stylish fashion, with expensive accessories, hats and jewelry. They were very hard to miss, and both served as walking advertisements for Hattie Wells' establishment. 55

The high-class nature of the Wells Waverly Place brothel, however, did not always guarantee good behavior from her customers, or her staff. There is no doubt that Wells aimed for higher standards than other establishments, but the very nature of the business meant that occasional customers, although appearing to be acceptable, could turn out to be otherwise.

In April, 1869 one of her new girls, Emma Seymour, had occasion to pull a pocket-knife on a patron named "Warner." She may have pulled the knife to defend herself as, according to other prostitutes at the Wells house, Warner tried to grab the weapon and Seymour sliced his hand, leaving him with a nasty wound. Warner had Seymour charged with assault, and she was immediately arrested by police. The matter was set for a court hearing the following day, but Warner failed to show and the case was dismissed. 56

In November, 1869 Emma Seymour was in trouble again, when a gambler known as "Dutch Charley" Rewitsky, alias Watkins, attacked her. Charley was a customer at the Wells brothel, and claimed Seymour was drunk and became violent toward him. He then attacked her and inflicted severe wounds to her face, arms, hands and legs. A fellow prostitute at the Wells house, named Mollie Clark, and the attending doctor, testified to the nature of the vicious assault that left Seymour "black, blue and yellow." If Hattie Wells' black porter was acting as a security guard, he had not been able to prevent the brutal assault, and "Dutch Charley" was held for trial in the police court. Three days later, he was found guilty of assault and the police prosecutor, Davis Louderback, insisted on a jail term, due to the brutality of the attack. As a result, "Dutch Charley" was sentenced to ten months in the county jail. 57

Even the owner of the establishment, Hattie Wells, was not immune to the dangers of the oldest profession. In October 1870, newspapers reported that Wells, a "fashionable member of the demimonde," and owner of a "high-end bagnio" at No. 3 Waverly Place was attacked by an unruly customer, named Dave McCarthy. He was charged with assault, having given Hattie a black eye. The exact circumstances that led to the attack were, unfortunately, not reported. This time, prosecutor Louderback dismissed the charges, but ordered McCarthy to pay the court costs. 58

One unsurprising fact about the entire industry was the high turn-over of staff in most establishments. No. 3 Waverly Place was no different. The 1870 federal census for San Francisco showed that none of the six women, who, in 1868, had traveled with Wells from

New York, were still listed at her brothel, twenty months later. Wells did not seem to restrict her girls, and they were free to come and go as they pleased, with some even visiting the State Fair in Sacramento. The unfortunate fact was there seemed to be plenty of newly arrived, willing women, or girls, to replace those who moved on, married, changed brothels, or died.

The 1870 federal census is instructive in terms of the ages and the individual wealth declared by the women at the Wells brothel. Hattie stated her age was 37 and her personal assets were valued at $5,000; Julia Clements aged 30, with assets of $2,000; Eva Lamont, aged 21, $1,000; Hattie Seymour, aged 20, $1,800; Molly (sic) Clark, aged 19, $500 and Minna "Minnie" Lee aged 17, listed without any assets – indicating she had probably just started out in the trade. These were large sums of money in 1870, and reflected the success of the establishment. 59

Business was so good that, by 1871, Hattie Wells leased a saloon nearby at 820 Clay Street, on the corner of Clay and Waverly. This was a small place, with only a couple of additional rooms, but may have been used to screen potential clients, or spot marks with money and then escort them, after a few drinks, to nearby No.3 Waverly Place.

It was at this time that a prostitute named Ella Howard began to work for Wells at Waverly Place. Like Florence Adams, Howard was more than likely a previous acquaintance of Wells from New York, or perhaps Chicago. She was known to own a very expensive array of gowns, dresses, and jewelry, which certainly qualified her for Waverly Place. Howard and Wells would then become close business associates. 60

In June, 1872 Wells again traveled to New York City, via the Isthmus of Panama, arriving there a month later on the steamship, *Rising Star*. This was the same

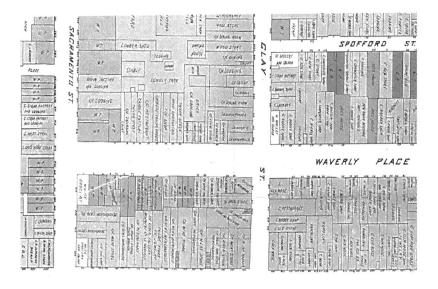

Waverly Place intersected with Sacramento Street and Clay Street. Hattie Wells ran the brothel at 3 Waverly Place, seen above, located next door to the white property on the lower corner of Waverly and Sacramento. She also ran a bar at 820 Clay Street, seen above, located in the white property on the upper corner of Clay and Waverly.

(Sanborn Insurance Map, circa 1885.)

vessel upon which she had sailed in 1868. The journey was probably for the purpose of recruitment, however, the results of this trip are not known, as the return-voyage passenger list was not reported in the San Francisco newspapers. 61

Despite her continued success, in February 1873, Hattie Wells decided it was time for a major change. She may have disliked the escalating violence and crime in the general area, or sensed the depression about to hit the American economy. In any case, she canceled her lease on both the Waverly Place and Clay Street addresses and sold all her fittings, fixtures and furniture, including her piano, at an auction held on February 28, 1873. Terms were "Cash in U. S. Gold Coin." The incredible array of expensive items highlighted the lavish standard of her brothel. It was easy to see how young women, from impoverished backgrounds, could easily be enticed into the wicked, yet luxurious, surrounds offered by Wells. 62

Prostitutes display themselves for selection in this posed photograph. (Courtesy of Aimee Crocker.com)

Auction Sales.

NEW FURNITURE At PRIVATE SALE
IN WAREROOM, OVER AUCTION ROOM.

SALE DAYS:

WEDNESDAYS and SATURDAYS.

FRIDAY.

FRIDAY.................February 28, 1873

AT 11 O'CLOCK A. M.,

ON THE PREMISES,

No. 820 CLAY STREET

—AND—

No. 3 Waverly Place,

WE WILL SELL THE

FURNITURE

—OF—

25 Elegantly Furnished Rooms,

Hattie Wells' 1873 auction advertisement.
Daily Alta (San Francisco) February 23, 1873.

50

COMPRISING IN PART:

One Very Elegant, seven-octave, Carved Legs, Rosewood Piano Forte, with Cover and Stool.

Elegantly Carved Rosewood Chamber Suits, Full Marble-tops;

Rosewood Single and Double Mirror Door Wardrobes;

Spiral Spring Mattresses, Curled Hair Mattresses;

Large Size French Feather Pillows, Mission Blankets;

New Style Body Brussels Carpets, Velvet Rugs;

Elegant Silk Brocat lle and Lace Curtains, with Gilt Cornices;

Carved Walnut Full Marble-top Chamber Suits;

Dressing Bureaus and Tables;

Clipper Lounges, Turkish Easy Chairs;

Elegant Gilt Frame French Plate Mantel Mirrors, Gas Chandeliers;

Oil Paintings, English Steel Line Engravings;

Vases and Ornaments;

Mahogany Marble-top Chamber Suits;

Rosewood Parlor Suit, Upholstered in Silk Brocatelle;

Rosewood and Walnut Marble-top Parlor Tables;

Walnut Plush Parlor Suits;

Walnut Marble-top Etagere;

Gilt Frame French Plate Pier Glasses, with Gilt Marble-top Base;

Parlor Desks, Walnut Hat Rack;

Gilt Toilet Sets;

Brussels Stair Carpets and Rods;

English Oil-cloths;

Walnut Marble-top Sideboard;

Extension Table, Dining Chairs;

China Dinner and Tea Sets;

Cutlery and Plated Ware;

Large Cooking Range, Copper Boiler;

Kitchen Furniture Complete;

Garden Hose, etc., etc.

Terms Cash in U. S. Gold Coin.

EDWARD S. SPEAR & CO.,
f25   **Auctioneers.**

Hattie Wells' 1873 auction advertisement.
Daily Alta (San Francisco) February 23, 1873.

51

When vacating Waverly Place, Wells took the bed linen with her but, unfortunately, a bundle of it fell from a removal wagon on Dupont, near Market Street, on the day of the auction. The linen must have been quite valuable, as Wells advertised for its return, stating a good reward would be paid to the finder, who was instructed to leave their name at the post office. 63

Hattie was fully cashed up after the auction, and decided to move her operations to Prescott, the former Arizona Territorial Capitol. The town was located in Yavapai County, among the picturesque Bradshaw Mountains, and was protected by nearby Fort Whipple. The community relied on gold and silver mining as its main sources of income. Accompanying Hattie Wells were Ella Howard and Florence Adams, the latter being one of the original women who had traveled with Wells from New York to San Francisco in October, 1868.

Hattie set up her new brothel on Granite Street, near Gurley Street, and went to work decorating and furnishing the place in expensive style. Her customers included politicians, merchants, doctors and a married former county sheriff named Johnny Behan. According to his divorce records, Behan had been a constant visitor to the Prescott brothels from about June, 1873, coincidently around the time that Hattie Wells set up her operations. 64

In April, 1874, the Yavapai County census showed that Wells was operating her Prescott brothel on Granite Street with six women, including her friend, Florence Adams, a 46-year-old of German heritage named Ameila Stevens, a new arrival known as Germima (sic) "Jennie" Andrews, who would play a small, yet important, role in an upcoming event, Mary Gardner, Lizzie Dunning and Millie Jordan. 65

Ella Howard had apparently set up her own small business, as she was listed near Wells' place on the 1874 census. Howard's brothel was much smaller, and apparently not as successful. She ended up owing $21.75 in delinquent taxes, and at 11:00 a.m., May 15, 1874, Howard's furniture was auctioned. Later that same day, she and her employee, another former Californian prostitute named Rosa Wakely, departed Prescott on the mail wagon, heading back to San Francisco, via Wickenburg and Los Angeles. 66

Four months later, Hattie Wells decided she needed a housekeeper, a servant and some fresh-faced younger women for her business. One of her married clients, Johnny Behan, had a liking for younger girls and had wed his already pregnant partner, Victoria, when she was only sixteen-years-old. Wells may have wanted to cater more to her clients' needs, and she knew one place to procure such young girls was in her old haunts, back in San Francisco.

On September 11, 1874, Hattie Wells followed her friend, Ella Howard, and took the mail wagon to Wickenburg, before traveling on to Los Angeles. As there was still no regular stagecoach in and out of Prescott, it was quite common for passengers to ride in the mail wagons, or buckboards. It was certainly not the preferred way to travel, but apparently it was usually quicker, if not as comfortable.

Eight days later, Wells had completed the 400-mile trip and booked into the impressive Pico House in Los Angeles. Two weeks later she was still living at the Pico House, as four letters, all addressed to Hattie Wells, were awaiting collection at the Los Angeles Post Office. The letters were addressed to her with four different salutations – "Mrs H. A. Wells; Miss Hattie Wells; Mrs Hattie A. Wells & Hattie Wells" – indicating that the correspondence was from multiple senders. Plans were clearly afoot. 67

The Pico House, Los Angeles, circa 1875.
(Courtesy California State Library)

6

EXIT JOSEPHINE "SADIE" MARCUS & ENTER "SADIE MANSFIELD"

Josephine "Sadie" Marcus [aka Marks] was never going to be content as a housekeeper, a cleaner, or a pupil, and she had no interest in marrying a Jewish merchant as had her half-sister, Rebecca. Josephine craved excitement and longed for a way to rid herself of the rules and the daily struggle she witnessed south of the Slot. She wanted the fancy dresses and jewelry she had seen women wearing at the Saturday matinees. She wanted the money you needed for that life-style and she wanted it sooner rather than later.

She had run away from home, without even a "goodbye," in September, 1873 and evidence suggests she had then been asked to take a job in another household, either to earn money for her family, or to keep her out of trouble. She was far too adventurous, bold and attractive for that plan to have ever worked. The shame and embarrassment she caused her family after her previous arrest, under her real name, would never happen again. She had learned a painful, yet very valuable lesson as a result.

The next time she ventured into the murky world of prostitution, it was under an alias. As Carol Mitchell and Roger Jay correctly concluded, the alias she used was "Sadie Mansfield." Her middle name was "Sarah," a Hebrew name meaning "woman of high rank," but was often replaced by "Sadie," being a less formal term of endearment used by her friends and her mother.

"Josie Mansfield" was the name of an infamous mistress of the day, who had made the headlines in newspapers across the country in the early 1870s. Josephine then simply combined her middle name with that of someone infamous, and "Sadie Mansfield" was born. This may have occurred soon after April, 1874 when she was still aged just thirteen, going on fourteen, which was seen as the prime age for some in the depraved San Francisco vice trade.

While Hattie Wells was staying at the Pico House in Los Angeles and organizing the recruitment of a housekeeper, a new working girl, and a servant, Ella Howard had been contacted and instructed to bring a new young recruit from San Francisco to Los Angeles. She chose Sadie Mansfield. There are no records available, as yet, to indicate how the two made initial contact. Given her age, Sadie may have already been willingly procured for a second time and started work, or been offered the Prescott job by Ella Howard while she was frequenting the Saturday matinees. Whatever the case, evidence indicates the pair commenced their trip from San Francisco, during bad weather, on or about October 25, 1874. 68

In her memoir, Josephine invented a story in which she was a schoolgirl who left home on a stormy day, carrying her school-books, but then ran away with her fictional schoolfriend, Dora Hirsch, in order to join the Pauline Markham performance troupe on their way to Arizona. Her incredulous story had lurched into an obvious lie to cover up the fact she was then only about thirteen years-old, by inserting herself into a theatrical tour that commenced five years later in October, 1879.

By doing so, she exposed her own attempted deception because, in 1879, she would have been eighteen years-old. As an adult, Sadie would have been free to come and go as she pleased, and certainly would not have been carrying books on her way to school.

Some authors, in an unconvincing attempt to make her story fit, have made the totally false claim that the two girls used the stage names of May Bell and Belle Howitt, (aka Hewitt) when they supposedly ran away with the Markham troupe. This claim is easily exposed as false, because the Markham troupe were all professional entertainers and both Mary "May" Bell and Belle Howitt were well-known actors, singers and performers who gave several individual performances in Tucson, in late 1879, with and without Markham.

MORA, *Belle Howitt.* 707 BROADWAY.

Professional actress and singer, Belle Howitt, sometimes spelled "Hewitt," toured with Pauline Markham in 1879. (Courtesy Library of Congress)

These performances were then reported and critiqued in the Tucson newspapers, and lauded for their quality, with special mention for Howitt and Bell.

In her memoir, Josephine actually mentioned rendezvousing with an "actress" downtown, before being taken to the docks to sail out of San Francisco Bay, as the main group had already left. In truth, the "actress" she met was Ella Howard, and evidence indicates the pair actually took a ferry across the bay to Oakland, from where they started their trip south.

Newspaper records show that "Mrs. Howard and Miss Mansfield, from San Francisco," later arrived at San Louis Obispo and booked into the Cosmopolitan Hotel. [69]

From there, "Mrs. E. Howard and Miss S. Mansfield, of San Francisco" continued south and arrived in Santa Barbara, staying at the Occidental Hotel on November 1, 1874. In her memoir, Sadie claimed to have stayed at the plush Arlington Hotel, in Santa Barbara, however, that was impossible as construction of that hotel was not completed and opened to the public until February, 1876. Ironically, Sadie would eventually visit the Arlington Hotel, but this would occur on a return trip.

From Santa Barbara, Ella Howard and Sadie Mansfield continued their journey, arriving at the Pico House to join Hattie Wells on November 5, 1874, as announced in the *Los Angeles Daily Star.* [70]

Pico House Advertisement, Los Angeles.
Los Angeles Herald, September 20, 1874.

Meanwhile, Hattie Wells had recruited a new working girl who used the alias, "Minnie Alice," and, more importantly for researchers, a black housekeeper, named "Mrs. Julia Burton," who sometimes went by the name of "Mrs. Julia Hubbard." *The Elevator*, a San Francisco newspaper specifically dedicated to news for black citizens, had reported her departure as "Mrs. Julia Hubbard for Arizona" in their edition dated October 31, 1874. [71]

Over the next week, Julia made her own way to the Pico House, in Los Angeles, to join the Wells entourage. She must have traveled independently of Ella Howard and Sadie Mansfield, as her name was not included on any hotel registers in San Louis Obispo, or Santa Barbara, for that same week.

7

"AUNT JULIA"

A careful study of Julia Burton's history is relevant to readers, as she was specifically mentioned by Josephine in her memoir, as "Aunt Julia," when she described their journey to Arizona.

The records show Julia was a black woman, born in Virginia, about 1820, and married to Claiborne Burton, also known as "Claiborne Hubbard," a black man, born about 1810, from Virginia, via Nashville, Tennessee. Why the couple chose to occasionally use two different surnames is yet to be determined. [72]

Records show that Claiborne Hubbard was working as a teamster in Mariposa County, California as early as 1852, without mention of a wife. He then moved to Sacramento, where he may have met Julia, and obtained a steady job, earning a decent wage of $50 per month, working as a porter and bootblack for the Sacramento Treasurer's Office. [73]

The couple were enumerated twice on the 1860 federal census in California. The first listing was in Sutter Township, on June 6, as "C. Hubbard" (black male) born 1817 (sic), Virginia; "Julia Ann Hubbard" (black female) born 1819, Virginia. [74]

On June 21, 1860, the pair were listed again; this time in Ward 2 of Sacramento City, as "Clayborn (sic) Hubbard" (black male) born 1810, Virginia; "Julia Hubbard" (black female) born 1820, Virginia. Interestingly, their next-door neighbors, on either side, were both prostitutes. 75

Throughout the 1860s, the couple used the "Hubbard" surname when leasing or purchasing property, and for listings in the Sacramento City Directory. 76

By May 1870, however, in accordance with the 15th Amendment to the U. S. Constitution, Claiborne registered to vote in Sacramento using the surname of "Burton," stating he was born 1807, in Virginia. He was one of the first black men to exercise his newly gained right to vote. Whether the name change, from Hubbard to Burton, was directly related to registering to vote, or related to previous unpaid debts is not known, but the couple maintained the "Burton" surname when the 1870 federal census was conducted. 77

They were enumerated on August 6, 1870 in Ward 2, Sacramento City, as "Claybourn (sic) Burton" (mulatto male) born 1807 (sic) in Virginia, working as a porter, with real estate valued at $500 and personal assets of $100; "Julia Burton" (mulatto female) born 1819 in Virginia, keeping house. Four other colored boarders occupied the same residence. Interestingly, the Sacramento City Directory for 1870, however, listed "Mrs Julia Hubbard" as a nurse at the same residence. 78

The alternating use of surnames continued when "Claiborne Hubbard's" death was announced in the *Sacramento Bee* on December 3 1870. This left Julia, in a dire financial state, yet when the bank foreclosed on their unpaid home mortgage, the newspapers noted, in 1871, that the property was owned by "Claiborne Burton and Julia A. Burton." 79

Julia, herself, also maintained use of the dual surnames, as she was listed as "Mrs. Julia Hubbard" when departing San Francisco in October, 1874, yet gave the name "Mrs. Julia Burton" when meeting up with Hattie Wells and Sadie Mansfield et. al. at the Pico House, in Los Angeles, less than a week later.

It is also important to note that the use of the dual surnames continued during Julia's subsequent life in Prescott, Arizona. The Yavapai County census, taken in 1876, listed her in Prescott at Hattie Wells' brothel as "Julia Hubbard," yet on a later Prescott federal census she gave her name as "Julia A. Burton," a widow.

She was commonly known around town as "Aunty Julia" and went on to be become a much loved and respected member of the Prescott community. So much so, that later, when taking a holiday, the Prescott *Weekly Miner* stated, "Aunty is well liked by every man, woman and child in this village, and they wish her good health and an enjoyable trip." 80

8

PRESCOTT,
ARIZONA TERRITORY

The recruitment of the negress housekeeper, "Aunt Julia" Burton, aka Hubbard, is a vital piece of information in regards to understanding how Josephine occasionally dropped her guard when dictating her memoir. She was not to know that researchers would, one day, carefully study her words and that those words would unmask the truth about her first trip to Arizona.

In her memoir, Josephine carelessly stated that her beautifully attired group of "actresses" were traveling by stagecoach with a negress maid known as "Aunt Julia." Hattie Wells' previous housekeeper in San Francisco had been a mulatto woman known as "Aunt Bess," so it is evident Wells typically preferred black women as housekeepers and cooks. 81

Josephine's fictional story of traveling with the Pauline Markham troupe, completely falls apart when a diligent study is made of Markham's entourage, and the actual route and mode of transport taken by that group to reach Arizona, five years later in 1879. Along with the star, Pauline Markham, was her husband

Randolph McMahon and additional male performers named Joe Dauphin, Tom Casselli, Frank Roraback and Harry Carpenter; female performers were Mary "May" Bell, Belle Howitt, sometimes spelled "Hewitt," and Gertrude Pring, aka "Gertrude Hayne." All members were Caucasian; males outnumbered females, and Pauline Markham did not travel with a maid. 82

The troupe actually operated on a tight budget, as the frontier venues were small in comparison to the large city theaters. The performers were multi-talented and would sometimes be required to portray different characters on any particular night. There were no inexperienced "extras," or "dancers," recruited for the tour. The troupe did not need them, and could not afford such luxuries on the frontier. If any additional crew, or stage attendants, were required, they were sourced from the local workforce in Tucson. The thought that professionals like Markham, Howitt and Bell, would tour with unknown and unskilled debutants was naïve. In addition, the Markham group traveled by train, not stagecoach, from Los Angeles to Yuma and then east to Casa Grande, near Tucson, Arizona. They did not travel directly to Prescott, and this information becomes very important when compared to the journey and route described by Josephine in her memoir. 83

Not only had Josephine incriminated herself in her memoir with the inclusion of the damning "negress, Aunt Julia" information, she then went on to describe the exact same route, and mode of transport, taken by Hattie Wells, "Aunt Julia" and the newly recruited prostitutes, to travel directly from Los Angeles to Prescott, in November, 1874. Those women were assembled at the Pico House, Los Angeles, and records suggest the group left the hotel on either the 6th or 7th of November, 1874 and traveled to San Bernardino.

Hattie Wells' substantial wealth then enabled her to charter a private stagecoach, in San Bernardino, to finish the road-trip, via Wickenburg, to Prescott. As Josephine recalled in her memoir, "We went by stage [from Santa Barbara] to Los Angeles and from there to San Bernardino. It was a strange and eventful life; I was living at close quarters with people who had always seemed like beings from another world... [it was no] time at all until we found ourselves boarding a stage at San Bernardino which was bound for Arizona." 84

Hattie, Sadie and the other ladies arrived in their private stagecoach at Wickenburg on November 18, after a tiresome, but uneventful, trip. Details of their full names, and their arrival and departure date from Wickenburg, were telegraphed to Prescott and printed in the local *Weekly Miner*, dated November 20, 1874 - "Miss Hattie Wells, Miss Ella Howard, Miss Saddie (sic) Mansfield, Miss Minnie Alice, Mrs. Julia Burton and servant." [the servant was probably Chinese, as no name was provided.] Sadie, then aged only thirteen or, at best, nearly fourteen, had arrived in Prescott. 85

In her memoir, Josephine desperately needed to hide her career as a runaway teenage prostitute, but in order to do so, she chose to embellish a lie so easily debunked that it is hard to understand how any reader, or writer, could mistake her sugar-sweet fairy-tale for the truth. She needed to somehow explain her previous association with Johnny Behan to her biographers. So, she went even further with her lie and claimed she met and fell for Behan during a chance encounter at a ranch, during the same trip, along the road to Wickenburg.

According to her, their group was delayed several days, due to marauding Indians, and the gallant and handsome Johnny Behan arrived at the same ranch, or stage-stop, where they met and exchanged flirtatious pleasantries. The whole story was nothing but a badly told fantasy, as the Wells group were not delayed, and Behan was not chasing Indians at the time. He was chasing votes, and was noted as arriving in Prescott on November 11, 1874 from the Little Colorado electoral district, which was to the north-east of Prescott, in the opposite direction from the road to Wickenburg. 86

The truth was that Sadie Marcus, then known as Sadie Mansfield, went straight to work at Hattie Wells' brothel on Granite Street, and one of her first and most enthusiastic clients was none other than Johnny Behan. He became so attracted to the young dark-haired, full-figured beauty, that he not only visited Hattie Wells' establishment and paid for Sadie's services, but also stayed overnight on more than one occasion during December, 1874. This luxury naturally incurred a much higher fee. Sadie was already good for the business. 87

Far from being the lost and reluctant home-sick runaway she claimed to be, Sadie was now a successful courtesan. She was living in luxury, with a steady income, and an enamored client named Johnny Behan, who happened to be financially secure, politically ambitious, but unfortunately married. In the memoir, she claimed he was "darkly handsome, with merry black eyes and an engaging smile and my heart was stirred by his attentions." 88

Prescott's notorious "Whiskey Row", which featured most of the town's saloons and gambling rooms.
(Courtesy Brad Courtney)

In reality, Behan did a lot more than that, and she may well have fallen for his charms and compliments in the same way that he was willing to pay for hers.

Only one incident marred Sadie's time in Prescott. It was the result of her participation in the "Grand New Year Gift Enterprise," which was a raffle supposed to take place after Christmas, 1874. Fifty prizes, valued at a total of $1,500, where up for grabs and mainly included men's and women's watches, jewelry, clocks and an array of decorative items, all of which were on display at the merchandise store of Asher & Co. Due to a lack of ticket sales, which cost $2 each, or six for $10, the draw did not actually take place until February 3, 1875.

As luck would have it, Sadie and one of her fellow prostitutes, Jennie Andrews, were listed as winners of principal prizes, being held at Asher's store. In what was probably a mix-up in regards to which of the major prizes she had actually won, Sadie picked up a set of silver German table-spoons from Asher's store. As they were not part of the prize package, Asher promptly had Sadie charged with petty larceny.

The spoons were located in her room at Hattie Wells' brothel by Sheriff Ed Bowers, and the matter was quickly brought to trial the same day, February 6, 1875. After hearing testimony from Sadie's fellow prostitute, Jennie Andrews, a five-man jury promptly found her "Not Guilty," and she was released. 89

Sadie purchased a winning ticket in the Gift Enterprise.
Weekly Miner (Prescott, Arizona) December 31, 1874.

In April, 1875, two letters awaited Sadie Mansfield at the Prescott Post Office. This seemingly innocuous mention is actually important because it meant she had at least one or two friends, probably from San Francisco, who knew her by her alias. One possibility was that Ella Howard was corresponding

70

with her from San Francisco, as newspapers indicate Howard had returned to that city during 1875. 90

The following month, Victoria Behan filed for divorce from her unfaithful husband, Johnny Behan, and specifically named Sadie Mansfield as the prostitute with whom he had spent more than one night at Wells' brothel. Victoria's divorce was granted, as she produced two witnesses who gave damning evidence to prove her case. The divorce was finalized on June 2, 1875, and Behan was then free to pursue youthful Sadie. Evidence, however, suggests he was more concerned with his political career. Behan used women, like Sadie, for his pleasure and his actions consistently showed he was not cut out for marriage. 91

It is important to note, again, that Hattie Wells did not restrict the girls in her employ, and it appears that Sadie returned to San Francisco during the summer of 1875. This may have been at the request of Ella Howard, who was working with another future infamous Arizona prostitute, named Minnie Powers. They were based out of Santa Barbara in 1875, and sailed aboard steamers between San Francisco, Santa Barbara and Los Angeles as a means to pick up and entertain wealthy clients.

When Sadie returned to San Francisco in 1875, it is not clear if she visited her family, as they had moved, once again, even further south of the Slot. Her father was then listed in the city directory as "Henry

Marcuse," a baker, at a very humble three-room dwelling at 10 Zoe Street. Her brother, Nathan, seemed to have retained the "Marks" spelling of his name and was listed as a laborer, working for the North Beach & Mission Rail Road. The national economic depression at that time had hit close to home, as her brother-in-law, Aaron Wiener, and his father, Isaac, officially petitioned the district court and declared themselves bankrupt, as of May 20, 1875. 92

Money may have been in short supply for her family, but it was no problem for Sadie. On November 1, 1875 she purchased a First-Class ticket and boarded the steamer *Mohongo,* setting sail from San Francisco, and arriving at Los Angeles the following day. Sadie was heading back to Prescott. 93

Her memoir would claim that she was "rescued" from the dangers of the wild frontier and left the Pauline Markham acting troupe, conveniently, without ever setting foot on the stage. She claimed to have been assisted in her return to San Francisco by a Prescott pioneer named Jake Marks, who she stated was a mutual friend of her bankrupt brother-in-law.

Once again, this was a complete fabrication. The Markham troupe were not in Prescott until Christmas, 1879, and Jake Marks, born in Kentucky, had spent most of his life in the goldfields, and on the frontier in Arizona and Nevada. He had no obvious connection to the Wiener family. Jake had sold his business and left

Prescott, with his wife, on February 5, 1876 to visit San Francisco. This was common knowledge to all in Prescott well before Jake left, and his involvement in any "rescue" of the runaway Sadie was just another fantasy, invented to cloud the facts. The truth was more interesting. 94

Sadie did leave Prescott again, but in late January, 1876 and she did not return for another four years. Hattie Wells then simply replaced her with another young prostitute known as "Willie Beatty." 95

A Prescott notable, named "Jeff" Davis, actually left Prescott with Sadie, the week before Jake Marks. The couple arrived in Los Angeles on February 7, 1876, and booked into the familiar Pico House, as "J. Davis & Miss Mansfield, Prescott." Newspapers then recorded the pair onboard the steamer, *Senator*, sailing from Anaheim, and stopping at all ports along the way to San Francisco.

They were recorded on the *Senator's* manifest, but changed their minds and stopped over at Santa Barbara to attend the grand opening festivities of the new Arlington Hotel. Records show they registered at the Morris House in Santa Barbara on February 11, as "Jeff Davis & Miss Mansfield, Prescott." Sadie was clearly in no hurry to be "rescued," and traveling by steamer and being named on the manifests of these ships, meant the couple had a First-Class cabin. Money was not a problem for Sadie and, in all likelihood, this was actually a courtesan and client relationship, with Davis probably paying the fares. The following day, the *Santa Barbara Morning Press* noted that the couple had booked a cabin and boarded the steamer *Orizaba*, sailing for San Francisco.

The steamship *Orizaba*, circa 1854.
(Courtesy San Diego History Center)

"Miss S. Mansfield and Jeff Davis" endured rough weather, but arrived safely the following day, Sunday February 13, 1876, as announced by the *Daily Alta*. Sadie had returned to San Francisco. 96

In her memoir, she claimed to have witnessed the gala premier of the Baldwin Theater on March 6, 1876, stating "it was certainly an event in my young life." Her arrival in San Francisco, the previous month, allowed for this possibility. Two weeks after the opening of the Baldwin Theater, a letter awaited Sadie Mansfield at the San Francisco Post Office. Once again, this detail is instructive, as it shows that she had informed friends, who knew her by her alias, of her new destination. Johnny Behan, her client from Prescott, looms as her likely correspondent, probably keen to obtain her new fixed address. 97

The Baldwin Theater and Hotel, circa 1879.
(Courtesy Mike Mihaljevich)

9

LURE OF THE LUCRE

When Sadie arrived home in San Francisco, her father was then listed in the 1876 city directory, under yet another name, "Henry Marcon," a baker, and still residing at No. 10 Zoe Street. Her brother, Nathan, was no longer listed in the city directory and, suspiciously, would not be included again for the next four years. He had either left the city or, perhaps, was doing time as an inmate in another correctional institution. 98

Despite her claims to the contrary, there is no guarantee that Sadie re-joined her impoverished family at No. 10 Zoe Street in 1876. Once a girl turned to high-class prostitution, it was very hard to break away from the lure of the big money on offer, and San Francisco certainly afforded a smart, young, attractive working girl many ways to make a good living "on the game."

One such example is the previously mentioned courtesan, Minnie Powers, who based her operations in Santa Barbara, but traveled to and from San Francisco, on steamers, to spend weekends away with selected clients. In these cases, the client's name was often suppressed, for obvious reasons, and recorded on ship manifests and hotel registers as simply, "Friend."

An example of this can be seen in the *Santa Barbara Morning Press* dated May 4, 1876, which stated that "Miss Powers & Friend" had boarded the steamer, *Orizaba*, in San Francisco, bound for Santa Barbara. On August 7, 1876, the *Orizaba* again left San Francisco and docked at Santa Barbara the following day. As it happened, "Miss Mansfield & Friend of San Francisco" then booked into the luxurious Arlington Hotel on August 8. This was the same hotel mentioned in her memoir when Sadie claimed to be on her way to Arizona. It was still under construction then but, this time, Sadie was finally able to enjoy its modern facilities and plush décor, albeit while on the job.

A few months later Sadie Mansfield was listed on the ship manifest of the steamer *Senator*, as leaving San Francisco bound for Los Angeles on January 24, 1877; it should be noted that this vessel stopped at Santa Barbara on the voyage south. 99

The steamship *Senator*, circa 1848.
(Courtesy mygoldrushtales.com)

The Arlington Hotel, Santa Barbara, circa 1876.
(Courtesy Santa Barbara Vintage Photography)

These examples tend to contradict the timing of the claim made in her memoir that, upon her return to San Francisco, she contracted a case of St. Vitus dance and was, "unable to attend school very much again." Her own confession of still being of school-age was, however, yet another nail in the coffin of her Markham tall-tale. The records suggest, if she did suffer from the ailment, it happened sometime after January, 1877. Likely it was then, in her time of need, when she could no longer work as a courtesan, due to the illness, that she reunited with her family. The symptoms of the disease could linger for up to two years and she actually confirmed this when she stated, "I gradually improved in health so that within two years of my experience, I was once again a normal healthy girl." 100

If Sadie did reunite with her family at the time of her sickness, it was at the cramped lodgings at No. 10 Zoe Street, where her father was listed in the 1877 city directory as "Henry Marcuse," a baker. This marked the third year in a row that the family had not been forced to move house. This may have been due to the low rent charged for the small three-room lodging, or the fact that Henry and Sophia had been supporting only their daughter, Henrietta, who was, by most accounts, a scholarly type, unlike her runaway sister and brother. Their bankrupt son-in-law, Aaron Wiener, was listed as a "Cigar Dealer," in 1877, residing at 138 Perry Street, a short walk from the Marcus household. 101

The return of Sadie may have been the catalyst for the family to move because, in 1878, for the first time in three years, they relocated to 244 Perry Street. The city directory listed "Henry Marcusa" as a baker at the new address and, once again, there was no listing for their son, Nathan, who was then 21-years-old.

The following year, 1879, could have been the time that Sadie recovered from her illness, as she claimed Johnny Behan, still smitten, paid her a visit from Arizona. The most likely time for this visit was in the first week of May, 1879. Behan had traveled, via Tucson, to Yuma on an unsuccessful hunt for a political appointment. He had his eight-year-old son, Albert, with him and wanted a specialist in San Francisco to assess his son's hearing loss.

While in San Francisco, he could have visited Sadie. How he knew where to find the Marcus family is open to speculation, as they were not listed in the 1879 city directory. In any case, according to her memoir, Behan came with a proposal of marriage. Having met and slept with him in Hattie Wells' brothel in 1874 and 1875, when he was still a married man, she should have known that he was not to be trusted. She did admit that "I was not at all sure that I cared enough for him to marry him, and so he returned to Arizona." It would not be long before she changed her mind. 102

John Harris Behan
(Courtesy Arizona Historical Society)

10

RUNAWAY - YET AGAIN

Later in 1879, Johnny Behan opened a saloon in the Arizona mining camp known as Tip Top, near the hamlet of Gillett, about 40 miles north of Phoenix. Tip Top was a crude camp full of miners, and what Behan needed was not a wife, but a working girl to potentially increase his business. According to restless Sadie, after denying his first request, he reached out to her again with another proposal, and this time she took the bait. She brazenly admitted, "Life was dull for me in San Francisco. In spite of my sad experience of a few years ago, the call to adventure still stirred my blood... I wanted the thrill of adventure and I was setting forth a second time [in truth, it was at least her third runaway] without my mother's consent or knowledge." 103

Why Sadie chose not to explain leaving home to her mother for a third time makes no sense, as she was now over eighteen years of age and free to live her life as an adult. Having deserted the family, causing them gross embarrassment and shame, when arrested in 1873, and then admitting to causing her mother extreme destress in relation to her second runaway in 1874, why would she repeat the dose for a third time?

81

If one reads between the lines, she failed to inform her mother as she had now fully recovered from her illness, and was ready to return to her former lucrative profession, with the bonus of Behan as a potential partner, rather than just a client.

Northen View of Tip Top, Arizona, circa 1888.
(Courtesy Arizona Pioneer & Cemetery
Research Project)

So, just like that, Sadie Mansfield, after a four-year absence, reappeared in Arizona at Gillett, the mill-site town that serviced the mining camp of Tip Top. She would then shadow Behan all the way to Tombstone. The *Phoenix Herald* dated February 13, 1880, reported Sadie's arrival from Gillett, and then reported Behan arriving there the following week, from Tip Top. After spending about ten days in Phoenix, Sadie Mansfield then traveled to Prescott, arriving there on March 2, 1880. She had been absent for four years, but some things had not changed. Her old employer, Hattie Wells, was still operating there on Granite Street, while "Aunt Julia" Burton was also in town, but now working as a housekeeper and carer for a prominent Prescott invalid pioneer, named Gideon Brooke.

Four days after her arrival, the Pauline Markham troupe, having been in Prescott for almost three months, performed songs and comedies before good crowds, charging a $1 entry fee. Given her love of the theater, Sadie was probably in the crowd, and it was these performances that may have planted the seed that led to her fantasy of being in the Markham troupe. 104

By June, 1880 the federal census showed Johnny Behan located back in Tip Top, and listed as a saloon keeper. Sadie had predictably joined him there, and was listed as a working girl. Behan's alleged desire to marry her had not eventuated, and Sadie was back doing what she seemed to enjoy. The census recorded her correctly as a nineteen-year-old courtesan, born in New York, with parents of German heritage. 105

Back in San Francisco, her family were not faring too well. Her brother-in-law, Aaron Wiener, had filed a petition of insolvency, in the Superior Court. He declared debts totalling $3,396, incurred while working in the family clothing business, but there were no assets that could be recovered to service the amount owed.

Sadie's brother, Nathan, had finally reappeared but, interestingly, was again living away from the family. He was then residing on Jackson Street, near Chinatown, only a couple of doors away from his family's original Powell Street address in 1870. 106

Times were so tough that Henry and Sophia Marcus and their daughter, Henrietta, had been forced to move in with bankrupt Aaron Wiener, his wife, and Wiener's four children. The 1880 federal census shows that the Wiener family were enumerated strictly by age with their father, Aaron, as the head of the family. The Marcus family then followed on the same census sheet with Henry (baker), Sophia (keeping house) and Henrietta, aged 17 (without occupation). Over the census page, and out of order, in terms of age, followed her brother, Nathan, aged 23, listed as a "laborer," and Josephine, aged 19, listed "at home."

As author Sherry Monahan noted, this was "a curious departure from normal census enumeration," and even more curious, given that the same enumerator had followed the correct procedure for the Wiener family in the same household. Some writers have used this information to question how "Sadie" could be listed in both San Francisco and Tip Top at the same time. The truth was that many parents still considered their absent children to be part of their family and gave census enumerators their names, even though they were not actually living at their home. This scenario played out in the Marcus household, as Nathan was listed in the 1880 San Francisco City Directory at a different address, and Sadie had run off to Tip Top to be with Johnny Behan. In her memoir, she mentioned that the true nature of her second runaway escapade had been kept private, and "friends were told I had gone away for a visit." This same ruse was, no doubt, used to then explain her third runaway. 107

Johnny Behan next moved to the boomtown of Tombstone in September 1880, but with one significant change in his circumstances. He had his nine-year-old son, Albert, with him. This change meant that Behan then needed a "wife" to assist with Albert's care, and it was at this time that Sadie reverted to her given name of Josephine, or Josie, and moved in with him. Her presence, as Josie, was documented only twice in Tombstone. A letter, was listed as waiting for "Josie Marcus" on April 16, 1881 in the *Tombstone Epitaph*. She stated in her memoir that she had written to her worried mother to advise of her new location, so the waiting missive was probably from her mother replying to tell her of the family's continued poor situation.

On June 11, 1881, trying to assist her family financially, a postal order for $25 was sent from Tombstone to "Mrs. H. Marcus" of San Francisco, by "Josephine Behan." This was one of only two references which indicated she had taken up with Johnny Behan in a common-law husband and wife relationship, but it did not last. On July 29, 1881 "Mrs Behan" exited Tombstone on the Kinnear stagecoach, and it seems her relationship with Behan also exited at the same time. She was headed back to San Francisco, as the *San Francisco Examiner* noted that "Mrs Behan of San Francisco" had passed Newhall, California by train, July 31, heading to the bay city. 108

It would seem that a friend from the demimonde in San Francisco, or Prescott, was still in contact, as a letter was listed for Sadie Mansfield at the Tombstone Post Office on August 13, 1881. If she failed to receive this letter, due to her return to San Francisco the previous fortnight, it did not seem to matter, as mail was later advertised for Sadie Mansfield in the *San Francisco Examiner* dated November 21, 1881. 109

Josephine "Sadie" Marcus left Tombstone (above)
on July 29, 1881 heading back to San Francisco.

11

THE GAMBLER

&

THE PROSTITUTE

Sadie returned to Tombstone early in 1882, and her travels can be easily traced through passenger reports which were published in both California and Arizona newspapers. The *Los Angeles Herald* noted that "Miss S. Mansfield, Tombstone" passed Fresno February 23, 1882, traveling by train, and would arrive in Los Angeles the following morning. The Tucson *Arizona Daily Star* then noted that "Mrs. (sic) S. Mansfield, Tombstone" had passed Colton, California and would arrive in Tucson, Arizona on February 25. The following day, the *Tombstone Epitaph* reported "S. Mansfield" had completed her journey from Tucson and booked into Brown's Hotel in Tombstone. 110

Her choice of accommodation was interesting, given the fact that Wyatt Earp had headquartered his entire family at the Cosmopolitan Hotel. Earp had deputized several gunmen to act as bodyguards for his brothers and their wives, in case of cowboy revenge attacks, and the Cosmopolitan had become a fortress for his family, including his common-law wife, 32-year-old, Celia Ann "Mattie" Blaylock. Coincidentally, "Mattie Earp, of Cedar Rapids, Iowa" was noted in the *Epitaph* as booking into the Cosmopolitan, only three days prior to Sadie's return to Tombstone. This mention implies that Mattie was returning from a trip, possibly to visit her remaining family in her home state of Iowa.

Brown's Hotel, Tombstone.
(Courtesy *True West* Magazine)

More importantly, a month after Sadie's return, on March 25, 1882, another money order was sent from Tombstone to assist her mother, "Mrs. H. Marcus," in San Francisco. The timing of the payment to her mother is of interest, as was her ability to pay for hotels and costly travel to and from Arizona by stagecoach and train. Sadie clearly had an income, yet her memoir never mentioned that she had ever worked a traditional job in her entire life. The only reasonable conclusion that can be drawn is that she was supporting herself, during this time, working as a courtesan. [111]

It is telling that Sadie's memoir is completely devoid of information about exactly how and when she met Wyatt Earp in Tombstone. The obvious inference, based on the previous conclusion, is that he met her via a courtesan and client relationship, or he simply noticed her in the course of her everyday life, on the game.

Wyatt's life had continually revolved around brothels, prostitutes, gamblers and saloons. This was the life he knew, and where he felt most comfortable. His common-law wife at the time, Mattie, was a former prostitute and it is, therefore, not surprising that he would come into contact with Sadie in the normal course of her work. In fact, it makes perfect sense.

The timing of her return to Tombstone, in 1882, was not ideal if her intention was to further her relationship with Earp. Cowboy revenge was ever imminent and Morgan Earp's eventual murder forced Wyatt to abandon Tombstone in late March, 1882. He then spent the better part of the next six months exiled in Gunnison, Colorado with his brother, Warren.

Sadie must have felt disillusioned by the tragic development, yet she lingered in town. On April 8,

1882, mail was advertised for "Sadie Mansfield" in Tombstone. She was then enumerated correctly in Tombstone, on the special Arizona Territorial Census, compiled in July, 1882 as "Sadie Mansfield," aged 21, and born in New York. Collectively, the mail, travel and census details confirm that from August 1881 to July 1882, she was known in both Tombstone and San Francisco, as "Sadie Mansfield;" and her only known source of income, under that name, was from prostitution. Wyatt, however, had far bigger problems, and once it became obvious that he would not be returning to Arizona, Sadie eventually gave up on Tombstone. She returned to her old haunts in San Francisco, sometime after July, 1882. 112

The entire Earp family's time in Tombstone had been cut short due to cowboy assassins. Wyatt's brother, Virgil, was left with a severely damaged arm when he was ambushed the previous December. He had remained in Tombstone with Wyatt, James and Warren until the murder of Morgan in March, 1882. Virgil then left Tombstone a few days later with his wife, Allie, and headed to his parent's home in Colton, California where Morgan's body would be laid to rest. Mattie Earp and James Earp's wife, Bessie, then traveled to Colton on March 24, 1882.

Virgil's left arm had been so badly damaged that he thought further surgery may be needed. So, he made his way, in May 1882, to San Francisco to seek expert advice and care, and probably a second opinion regarding any further possible surgical treatment. 113

The outcome of his medical care was not made public, but Virgil must have liked the city and its apparent money-making opportunities, particularly in regards to gambling. The *Los Angeles Herald* heard news of his travels and reported, in July, 1882 that Virgil had started a business in San Francisco. 114

The business, of course, was faro, and Earp had opened a gambling den, located on the second floor at 15 Morton Street. The street was infamous for its seedy brothels and gambling rooms. It was the domain of the demimonde, and Virgil was back in the Earps' element. He then employed a former Tombstone faro dealer named Willis Lawrence, who had previously worked with Doc Holliday at the Alhambra Saloon. 115

A reporter from the *San Francisco Chronicle* visited the Earp clubrooms and described the "Tiger's Lair" as having a front door fitted with a burglar or police alarm; thickly carpeted stairs that led to a second story and a knob-less door, in which a four-inch cut had been made, so that a look-out could screen any visitors and "watch over the tiger's fortunes." 116

No sooner had Virgil opened the doors to the Morton Street faro rooms, a major police raid was conducted. The *San Francisco Chronicle* noted that raids were carried out on nine establishments on the evening of August 1, 1882. The first joint to be hit, and hit hard, was the Earp's clubroom at Morton Street. The *Chronicle* told the story:

At 15 Morton Street, the posse under Sergeant Bethel broke in the door and ascended to the second story, where the gambling rooms are located, and succeeded in arresting fifteen persons and in capturing the entire layout of checks, boxes, cards, etc., and $1422 in cash. The game at this place was conducted by Virgil Earp, a member of the notorious Earp family of Arizona, who carried his arm in a sling from the result of some recent fracas. 117

Virgil Earp paid bail of $200 for himself and $40 a head for all his arrested patrons. Coupled with the loss of $1422 – the most of any joint on the night – and all the playing equipment, the raid had been a very expensive inconvenience for Virgil. Undeterred, he maintained the lease on the Morton Street location, but spent the next month in Colton, allowing his left arm to further heal as best it could.

Evidence suggests Virgil then corresponded with his younger brother, Warren, in Colorado, as mail was advertised for "Warren B. Earp," September 4, 1882 in the *Gunnison Review Press*. Wyatt and Warren were making plans to end their exile in Colorado and return to California. Virgil then left his wife, Allie, in Colton and returned, by train, to San Francisco, September 21,

1882. One month later, he would reunite in Sacramento with Warren and Wyatt. The *Sacramento Daily Record-Union* of October 20, 1882 noted that Virgil had come to town to meet his brother, "W. B. Earp, who will arrive from the East this morning." This reference was to his brother, Warren Baxter Earp, as Wyatt was taking no chances and made the trip under the alias "W. B. Stapp." A Western Union telegram, probably sent by Virgil to coordinate their meeting, had awaited Wyatt under that alias in Salt Lake City, Utah on October 15, 1882, as mentioned in the *Salt Lake Herald.*

Interestingly, when Warren and Wyatt made the journey from Gunnison to Sacramento, Warren Earp was accompanied by a woman listed as his wife but, who in all probability, was a prostitute heading to California. The *San Francisco Chronicle* had reported "W. B. Earp and wife" of San Francisco, [Warren] along with "W. B. Stapp" of Salt Lake, [Wyatt] passed Carlin, Nevada to arrive in Sacramento, California as of October 20, 1882. 118

The brothers had much to discuss and plan in regards to accommodation and the Morton Street faro den. They appear to have lingered in the area for ten days, before heading home to Colton, California. The *Los Angeles Herald* then reported the three brothers, V. W. Earp, W. S. Earp and W. B. Carp (sic) [Warren Earp] passed Fresno heading south on October 31, 1882. There was no mention of the woman who had traveled with Warren Earp to Sacramento, indicating she must have stayed in Sacramento, or completed the trip to San Francisco. 119

When Wyatt arrived at the home of his parents, in Colton, November 1, 1882, his wife Mattie was not there to greet him. Evidence suggests she grew tired of living without Wyatt in Colton, and decided to embark

Celia Ann "Mattie" Blaylock, circa 1871. She was Wyatt's common-law wife at the time he met Sadie. (Courtesy Arizona Historical Society)

on a trip of her own. A newspaper report suggests she may have journeyed back to Cedar Rapids, Iowa to visit with her mother, Elizabeth "Betsy" Blaylock, and her married sister, Sarah Marquis. Both women lived as neighbors, just outside Cedar Rapids, and it is hoped they greeted her warmly. If so, Mattie should have stayed with them as, unbeknown to her, Wyatt had no intention of continuing their marriage. Mattie was noted as returning to California, November 15, 1882 as reported in the *Sacramento Daily Record-Union*, "Mrs. Mattie Earp, Salt Lake City" had passed Carlin, Nevada to arrive in Sacramento the same day. It is more than likely, by the time Mattie reached Colton, Wyatt had already left for San Francisco, which would then be his home for the next five months.

Sadie, meanwhile, still required an income, and continued plying her trade on the steamers, up and down the Pacific coast. She sailed with another woman named May Smart, on October 30, 1882, from San Francisco to Olympia, Washington. It is possible that "May Smart" was actually a 20-year-old prostitute, originally from California, who went by the name of "Clara Smart" in Tombstone. Clara Smart had been enumerated, along with Sadie Mansfield, in Tombstone during the Arizona Territorial Census, July 1882. 120

In November, 1882 the four remaining Earp brothers, including James, came together in San Francisco to headquarter their business operations at the Morton Street faro establishment. The brothers rented furnished residential suites at a rooming house at 604 Pine Street in San Francisco. Wyatt, Virgil and Warren were all listed at that address in the 1883 San Francisco City Directory. 121

It was during the period from November, 1882 to March, 1883 that Sadie finally gave up the game, and her alias, "Sadie Mansfield," disappeared from the records. She became "Sadie Earp" and commenced a full-time relationship with Wyatt in San Francisco. In all probability, Sadie lived with Earp at 604 Pine Street during this period. She may also have assisted with the operations of the Earp faro rooms at 15 Morton Street, as the prostitution conducted on the same street would not have concerned her at all.

It is possible that a piece of fine jewelry, that went missing from Morton Street, belonged to Sadie. Wyatt used the Morton Street address when he placed an advertisement for the missing ring in the *San Francisco Chronicle,* dated January 11, 12 & 13, 1883, "Lost – Diamond Ring containing three diamonds, Suitable reward on return to W. S. Earp, 15 Morton Street." (see below)

LOST – DIAMOND RING CONTAINING three diamonds. Suitable reward on return to W. S. EARP, 15 Morton street.

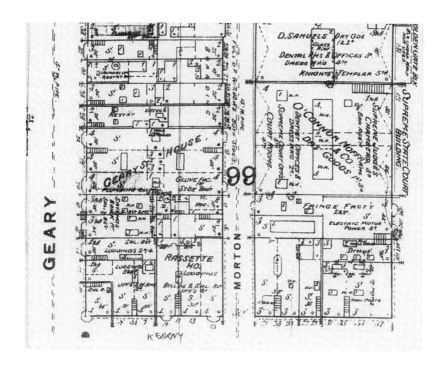

The Geary House backed onto the Earp brother's faro den at 15 Morton Street. See above, to the left of the number "99" on Morton Street. Players and employees could escape via the Geary House, to avoid arrest, if news of a police raid was received in time. (Sanborn Insurance Map, circa 1885.)

The next significant report of a police raid on gambling in San Francisco came in early March, 1883 and it was noticeably aimed straight at the location of the Earp's premises. The police focussed directly on Morton Street and, on the night of March 10, they hit a game at No. 21, before attempting to gain access to the Earp clubrooms down the street. This time, the brothers

97

had been warned and closed the faro bank and left the place, via the rear entrance on Geary Street, in enough time to avoid arrest. 122

This raid seemed to mark the beginning of the end for the Earp brothers in San Francisco. Virgil's wife, Allie, traveled from Colton to join her husband in San Francisco on March 18, 1883, but they enjoyed only two weeks together before heading south. The police raids appear to have taken their toll, as Virgil, Allie and Warren headed back to Colton, California on April 2, 1883, where James would run a saloon. 123

Wyatt was on the move too. He deserted Mattie, and left her to fend for herself in Colton. She would never recover, and later claim he had ruined her life. Earp's ultimate destination was Silverton, Colorado, another booming mining camp, high in the Rockies. The railway connecting Silverton to Ouray, Colorado had been completed in July, 1882 making it an easier destination for gamblers and saloon-men to reach. The *Sacramento Daily Record-Union* reported that Wyatt Earp passed through their city on April, 5 1883, heading east for a stop in Utah, on his way to Silverton. No mention of a wife, or woman, was included, suggesting that Sadie was not with him at this time. 124

The Salt Lake City, Utah *Herald* confirmed Wyatt's arrival there as of April 6, 1883. He booked into the Walker House, alone, with no mention, or reference to Sadie, or any female companion. 125

Wyatt's journey into Colorado can be further traced, as he passed through the mountain town of Ouray. *The Solid Muldoon* noted his arrival in their town during the week ending April 20, 1883. Again, there was no mention of Sadie, or a wife, traveling with him. The newspaper mentioned he was on his way to Silverton, and stated "Mr. Earp looked anything else but the man Arizona journalists have pictured him." 126

Silverton, Colorado, circa 1880.
(Courtesy westernmininghistory.org)

Three separate primary sources failed to mention Sadie, as Wyatt made his way to Silverton, Colorado. This begs the question as to whether she was actually with him during this period? In her memoir, regarding their subsequent travels together, Sadie did specifically mention their first stop was Salt Lake City, and that they stayed for a short time. However, the chapter devoted to this period of her life is hopelessly muddled in regards to chronology. She does state later that she and Wyatt passed through Ouray, Colorado on their way to Silverton, so some credence must be given to those reflections, as they do fit with Wyatt's known movements. However, Sadie claimed the pair tried to travel by buckboard, in a heavy snow, from Ouray to Silverton, which makes no sense, as the two towns were connected by rail. If she was being truthful about their location, if not their mode of transport, it is hard to imagine how her presence was not recorded, or mentioned, by reporters during the entire trip. 127

Another inconsistency in her memoir related to her reflections of an incident, during this period, which would become known as the "Dodge City War." Sadie separated this incident from her previous mention of Silverton, which tends to imply she may have been simply repeating information she had read, rather than something she had experienced. 128

The Dodge City incident occurred about a month after Wyatt had arrived in Silverton. Earp, and several other gamblers, were called into action to assist Luke Short, who was having trouble in Dodge City, Kansas. He had been ousted from his saloon, and arrested, during a political play by his opponents, who wanted Luke gone from Dodge. Wyatt and a posse of Colorado gunmen traveled to Dodge City, in a show of force, that helped turn the tide in favor of Short. No shots were fired and, collectively, Wyatt and his friends were christened the "Dodge City Peace Commission."

Once again, all reports of the affair failed to mention Sadie, or "Mrs. Earp," as traveling with Wyatt, and it made no sense for her to have been there, in any capacity. Yet, she claimed she was, and stayed in a small hotel, out of the way, during the tense stand-off. In her memoir, however, Sadie lapsed into a nostalgic retelling of Wyatt's time in Dodge City from the 1870s, which tends to suggest she was merely repeating sections of Stuart Lake's biography of Wyatt Earp. 129

The famous Dodge City Peace Commission photograph (above) was probably taken circa early June, 1883. It is an important image, as it shows how Wyatt Earp (seated front row, second from the left) appeared during the time Sadie first became acquainted with him.
(Courtesy *True West* Magazine)

By June 10, 1883 Wyatt and Bat Masterson had left Dodge City and were noted as stopping in Garden City, Kansas. The pair of gamblers then returned to Silverton, Colorado, arriving there by June 15, 1883 according to the Topeka, *Daily Commonwealth*. 130

Again, there was no mention of Wyatt traveling with Sadie, or with a wife. If she did accompany him on these early adventures, she did so in the shadows. She was kept well out of the public eye, and that of the local press, at these various places.

Back in San Francisco, Sadie's sister, Hattie Marcus, was living the life of a prim and proper, albeit poor, young Jewish lady. Hattie was the antithesis of her sister, Sadie. She had remained a dutiful daughter, had attended school, cared for her parents and eventually met Emil Lehnhardt, a skilled Jewish watchmaker, who had worked his way up to become the manager of a jewelry company. Emil was a hard worker, and the kind of man any parent would be pleased to welcome into their family. He lived with his parents, noticeably north of the Slot, in a much better area than Hattie and Sadie had known as young girls.

Emil and Hattie probably courted for a suitable period, before the 26-year-old Lehnhardt married 20-year-old Hattie Marcus in San Francisco, on July 5, 1883. The couple then moved into their own home at 615 Gough Street, San Francisco, still close to his parents, who were only a couple of blocks away. 131

Henrietta "Hattie" Marcus Lehnhardt (above) was
Sadie's generous younger sister, circa late-1880s.
(Courtesy of the Macartney family)

Whether Sadie was present for her sister's wedding is open to debate. There are no records of Sadie arriving in San Francisco for the occasion, and she did not mention anything about the wedding in her memoir. It is highly doubtful that Wyatt would have made the trip back to San Francisco, so we are left to ponder if Sadie made the trip alone, or if she made the trip at all.

In fact, the first public indication that Sadie and Wyatt were actually traveling together would be a hotel arrival notice in the *Salt Lake Herald*. The newspaper announced that "Wyatt Earl (sic) and wife, of Gunnison," had booked into the New Metropolitan Hotel, on August 29, 1883. The mention of "Gunnison" suggested the pair were heading west, rather than east from California. Interestingly, three weeks later, a letter was advertised in the "ladies list," for "S. Earp" at the Salt Lake City Post Office. This implied the couple remained in Utah for an extended period. 132

November, 1883 found Wyatt back in Dodge City, Kansas during the local elections. From there, he and Sadie joined with Johnny "Crooked Mouth" Green and his "wife," and the two couples embarked on a three-month gambling tour. Green had been with Wyatt during the so-called "Dodge City War," and was a professional gambler and firm friend. The foursome traveled to Texas, and were noted in *The Galveston Daily News* of December 1, 1883 as booking into the

Washington Hotel in Galveston – "J. R. Green and wife, Denver; W. S. Earp and wife, San Francisco." They may have enjoyed an extended stay in Galveston, as two items of mail were listed, awaiting Sadie's collection, during the week ending December 22, 1883. One letter was addressed to "Mrs. Josephine Earp," with the other addressed to "Mrs. Sadie Earp." [133]

The Washington Hotel, Galveston, Texas.
Wyatt & Sadie stayed at the hotel in December, 1883.
(Courtesy Galveston-History.blogspot.com)

This trip would be typical of the life that Sadie faced with Wyatt. For better or worse, the former prostitute and the gambler became life-long partners. "Sadie Earp," as she was steadfastly known, until Wyatt's death, had successfully hidden her past and defiantly refused to reveal the truth about her life during the period 1870 to 1883.

Ironically, it was the holes she left in her story, and the careless inclusion of some very incriminating information, that prompted diligent researchers to eventually dig up the truth that she tried so hard to bury. As Sadie, herself, commented in her memoir, "a thoughtless remark is like a pebble thrown into a pool. The ripples it creates spread and widen." Sadie's own words would prove to be prophetic. 134

While dictating her false claims of joining the Pauline Markham troupe to Mabel Earp Cason, Sadie feared some old-timers, who knew the truth of her career as a prostitute in San Francisco, Prescott and Tombstone, may have already mentioned the fact or, at least, alluded to her less than savory past.

In order to discredit any such unwanted revelations, Sadie continued to blur the truth and maintained her ruse of merely being a runaway "would-be dancer." She pre-emptively commented, "it is impossible to really keep any incident secret. The world is small after all, and at various times, and in divers [several] places, I have heard it whispered that, before my marriage, I was a dancer. The rumors placed [my] dancing career all the way from the Bird Cage Theater in Tombstone, Arizona to a dance hall in Nome, Alaska." Even in old-age, when looking back at the reality of that unsavory period of her life, it appeared she was still badly haunted by her memories. She openly stated, "even to this day, the whole experience recurs to my memory as a bad dream." 135

Any assessment of her life must conclude that Sadie obviously fared much better than her fellow 1873 runaways, Lizzie McCloud and Katy Cassidy. Unlike those unfortunate girls, and many others like them, she had survived her life as a prostitute. Sadie seems to have also avoided the drug and alcohol addiction that plagued many prostitutes of the era, so, she could certainly be considered a true survivor, in that regard.

It is not known if she ever suffered any physical violence or disease, which were typical occupational hazards of the flesh-trade at that time. As previously mentioned, she did claim to suffer a case of St. Vitus dance as a result of her experience, but there can be little doubt the lifestyle also left her with much emotional guilt. It is this author's opinion that Sadie was sincere when she commented, "the memory of it has been a source of humiliation and regret to me in all the years since that time." This strongly worded language wreaks of remorse, and more accurately reflects the serious nature of her true indiscretions. 136

JEFFREYS LEWIS.

Bat Masterson claimed Sadie Earp was very similar
in looks to the famous actress, Jeffreys Lewis.
(Courtesy Library of Congress)

THE TRUTH, OR
"A NICE, CLEAN STORY"

When Sadie Marcus chose Wyatt Earp as her life-long partner, she knew exactly what she was getting. She had seen him in action in both Tombstone and San Francisco, and knew he already had a "wife," whom he pragmatically, and coldly, deserted in her favor. Sadie knew he was an itinerant gambler, who was constantly looking for the next big score. He was at home in frontier boom-towns, at gambling tables and race-tracks, or staking mining claims, in the constant hope of striking it rich. This, then became her life too.

The couple lived in hotel rooms, and traveled the country, far and wide, on wagons, stagecoaches, trains and steamships and, as a result, owned very little in the way of worldly possessions. They spent their money as fast as they made any, never thinking of the future, beyond the next turn of a card, or result of the next race.

It was an exciting life, while they were both young enough to enjoy the wins and absorb the losses. It was the "wild ride" she had coveted ever since she was twelve-years-old, and she had found a man who shared her own desire to live without the restraints of a permanent home, a steady job, and the responsibilities that came with them. Wyatt was about thirteen years her senior, so it would come as no surprise that Sadie often proved to be a handful for the aging gambler. In fact, their relationship was, at times, far from perfect. Sadie was a strong-willed woman, who gave as good as she got, and their problems were only exacerbated as they grew older, and her looks and figure faded.

Wyatt's life was typical of many gamblers of the era. As the frontier slowly became civilized, and the boom-towns dried up and blew away so, too, did his ability to run gambling dens. Major cities had regular attacks of civic conscience, and routinely shut down gambling rooms, so Wyatt turned his hand to race-horses. The couple then traveled the country with some very successful, and not so successful, horses. At least this form of gambling was legal, although, like all contests involving gamblers, it was open to corruption – something with which Earp was very familiar.

Sadie was amused and enticed by the "Sport of Kings" and the race-track lifestyle, which included the advantage of rubbing shoulders with wealthy money-men like Elias "Lucky" Baldwin and Lew Rickabaugh.

The money flowed while some of his horses were winning, but the cost of finding and keeping a stable of competitive horses was high, and Wyatt would eventually leave the business without much to show for it. Sadie, on the other hand, developed a gambling habit that proved hard to shake, and even harder to afford.

Wyatt and Sadie even went to Alaska, chasing the thrill of the last of the frontier's big mining booms. Predictably, Wyatt ran a saloon to mine the miners, allegedly with great success. When the couple returned to the mainland, Wyatt went straight back into the saloon business – this time in remote Tonopah, Nevada.

The cracks in their relationship were exposed in Tonopah, where Wyatt was said to have knocked Sadie down at a gambling table. This rumor gathers weight when combined with newspaper reports, showing Sadie left Earp in Tonopah, on several occasions, to visit with her sister and mother in Oakland, California.

The cycle of highs and lows eventually caught up with the couple in their older age. Without savings, or a decent home to call their own, they spent Wyatt's twilight years living in cheap rental accommodation in Los Angeles, while also working mining claims south of Needles, California. He was still searching for the last big bonanza, but it would never eventuate.

As the moving-picture industry developed and Hollywood took shape, an elderly Wyatt decided to tell his life story, in the hope of setting the record straight, and making a buck or two.

Stuart Lake agreed to write his biography, but Wyatt would never see the finished product, as he died January 13, 1929, two years before the book's eventual publication in 1931. Sadie fought tooth and nail with Stuart Lake to keep her name out of the book, declaring it had to be a "nice, clean story." Her inclusion in the book would have made it the complete opposite, and she knew it. Her appearance in the text would have raised difficult questions that Sadie had no interest in answering, and which might have exposed the period of her life she desperately wanted to keep hidden.

Sadly, Sadie did not attend Wyatt's funeral, but a few of his surviving friends from their Tombstone days did. She claimed to be too sick and distraught to attend, but perhaps simply did not want to face Wyatt's former associates who might have remembered the truth.

She would eventually rely on her wealthy sister, Hattie Lehnhardt, to make ends meet. When Hattie died in 1936, she was left to fend for herself. Sadie's high-risk lifestyle with Wyatt had certainly provided her with the excitement she craved, but when it was all over, she was left with empty pockets, and a hatful of secrets and regrets.

The evidence of her deep regret was stated openly in her memoir. It is clearly seen in the fantasy tales she felt compelled to invent, in order to hide her scandalous years as a teenage prostitute; a situation entirely of her own choosing.

Her fictional stories, however, were then woven into the very fabric of the "Earp" legend, and have been perpetuated in big-budget movies, and some poorly researched books. The truth was sacrificed, just as Sadie had intended.

PROVEN IMAGES

It is very important to note that no proven photographs have been found, to date, of Josephine "Sadie" Marcus, aka Sadie Mansfield, aka Sadie Earp, during the period, 1870 to 1883. The internet is awash with photographs claiming to be Sadie in her younger years but, as of 2024, no such photographs, with any provenance, have been verified.

One reason for the lack of any verified youthful family photographs of Sadie was probably the result of the poverty in which she was raised. This theory gathers strength when one considers there are no known photographs of her mother and father, Sophia and Hyman Henry, or her half-sister, Rebecca, brother Nathan, or sister Henrietta "Hattie," individually, or as a family, during their poorest years.

Any images of Sadie as a prostitute, during the years 1873 to 1882, if they ever existed, may well have been destroyed by her later, during admitted moments of deep regret, in an effort to keep what she saw as a shameful period of her life away from public scrutiny.

To date, no photographs of Wyatt and Sadie, together as a younger couple, have been located or presented with any provenance, or direct links to the Earp, or Marcus families.

Wyatt Earp's most famous portrait, seen above, was taken during the mid, to late 1880s. No proven image of Sadie, taken during this time-frame, has been located to date.

(Courtesy Craig Fouts)

Even more intriguing is the fact that her wealthy sister, Hattie, did not seem to keep any photographs of her sisters, her brother, or her parents.

In the case of Sadie and her brother, Nathan, this may well have been the result of them both having run away from home at a very early age. Both Sadie and Nathan then spent the remainder of their lives constantly on the move, meaning neither were around if, or when, family photographs may have been taken.

Wyatt's most famous portrait was taken in San Diego, in the mid to late 1880s, yet no portrait of Sadie has survived, or surfaced, for the same period.

Some previous authors, and their publishers, have shamelessly included photographs of random women, suggested to be Sadie, on their covers, that have no proven connection to the Earp, or Marcus, families and absolutely no historical provenance to justify their use. Desperate to please or titillate readers, more dubious images of various young women have also been included within the pages of some publications. By doing so, these publications not only perpetuated untruths about Sadie's life from 1870 to 1883, they also helped to suggest validation of those same unproven images.

Unfortunately, for genuine historians, this has created a "free-for-all" situation, where the release of faked and fraudulent photographs, said to be Wyatt or Sadie, has become a regular occurrence. Powered by the internet, these images have then been shared and published online with reckless abandon. So much so, that they are eventually thought, by the ill-informed, to be real.

In the interest of accuracy, the image on the cover of this publication, along with the image on page 8, and those which follow, are some that have been verified. All the images of Sadie were taken in the 20th century, when she was at least over fifty years of age.

Sadie and Wyatt camping at their mining claim, west of Parker, near the Colorado River, circa mid-1910s. The stark contrast to her sister's wealthy lifestyle was obvious. (Courtesy Wild West History Association)

EMIL LEHNHARDT.

(Oakland Tribune, June 2, 1904.)
Emil Lehnhardt was Sadie Earp's wealthy brother-in-law.
He started a candy and ice-cream business in Oakland, in
1887, and achieved hard-earned success and popularity.

NEW HOME OF EMIL LEHNHARDT.
(*Oakland Tribune*, May, 21, 1904.)

In early 1904, Emil Lehnhardt commissioned an architect
to design the above mansion, which was to be built later
the same year on Telegraph Avenue, in Oakland, CA. He
and Hattie and their two children lived at the Albany Hotel,
in Oakland, during the construction period. They moved
into the impressive home in September, 1904. Sadie's
brother, Nathan Marcus, died at this home on May 17,
1906. In the 1930 federal census, the home was valued at
$75,000. One wonders how Sadie and Wyatt felt when
they visited Hattie and her family at the palatial home, and
if they each ever questioned their own choices in life, while
living in a tent at their remote mining claim. Sadie had
always been preoccupied with living an exciting, carefree
life, while Wyatt spent his entire time chasing his elusive
dreams of wealth at faro tables, race-tracks, mining claims,
and in smoky saloons, from Arizona to Alaska.

(Oakland Enquirer, January 16, 1911.)

Emil H. M. Lehnhardt Jnr., seen above in fancy-dress, was
Hattie Lehnhardt's son, and Sadie Earp's nephew. He was
born May 24,1902 and passed away October 31, 1943.

Emil Lehnhardt

(*San Francisco Call*, January 27, 1912.)

Sadie Earp's brother-in-law, Emil Lehnhardt, seen above, minus his mustache. He shocked the community and his family and friends when, despite his financial success, he took his own life by shooting himself in the right temple, January 26, 1912 in Oakland, California. He left his family an estate valued at over $225,000 and a thriving business.

Wyatt S. Earp, circa late 1920s.
(Courtesy *True West* Magazine)

Josephine "Sadie" Earp, circa late 1920s.
(Courtesy John Boessenecker)

Wyatt S. Earp, seen above in a pensive mood, during the late 1920s, at home in Los Angeles. He passed away there January 13, 1929, aged 80. His legend, however, was just taking shape and, thanks to his biographer, Stuart Lake, would continue to grow and enthral readers, researchers and writers for the rest of the 20th century, and well beyond.

(Courtesy *True West* Magazine)

(*Oakland Tribune*, April 8, 1936.)

Henrietta "Hattie" Marcus Lehnhardt managed her late husband's candy business for 17 years. She died April 7, 1936, leaving her older sister, Sadie Earp, without support.

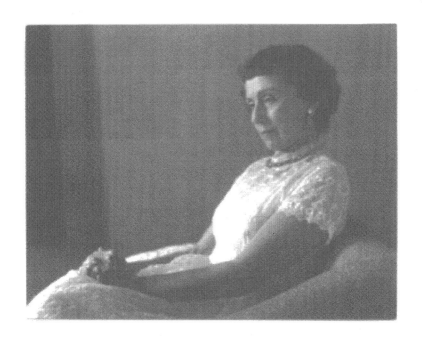

Edna Lehnhardt (above) was Emil and Hattie Lehnhardt's only daughter, and Sadie's niece. She was present at her parent's lavish 25th Wedding Anniversary Party, held at their beautiful home on Telegraph Avenue, Oakland, on July 4, 1908. Her aunt and uncle, Rebecca and Aaron Wiener, were part of the invitation-only celebrations. Noticeably, Sadie and Wyatt Earp were not included on the guest list. When Edna celebrated her own wedding in Oakland, on October 28, 1908, Sadie and Wyatt were, once again, left off the invitation list. By 1917, however, Edna had become closer to the Earps, and traveled on several occasions with Sadie to visit Wyatt's mining claims, west of Parker, Arizona. Edna would marry three times during her long life. Her large inheritance allowed her to study art, and she is remembered today as a painter, who specialized in colorful impressionist pieces. She died in 1966, while holidaying in San Luis Potosi, Mexico.

(Courtesy Bancroft Library, California)

Vinnolia Earp Ackerman (left) and Sadie Earp (right), in 1937, during a road-trip to Tombstone and Mesa, Arizona. This photograph was taken at "Earp," in eastern California. (Courtesy Jeanne Cason Laing)

Josephine "Sadie" Earp, seen here on the far left, with the Cason family. Mabel Earp Cason stands in the middle with her husband. Their daughter, Jeanne Cason Laing, stands on the far right. Mabel Earp Cason had housed and cared for Josephine while trying to write her memoir. The ambitious project was abandoned not long after this photograph was taken, circa 1940. Josephine "Sadie" Earp died, December 19, 1944 in Los Angeles. Mabel was a gifted artist whose Western Wildlife sketches were featured, weekly, in the *Oakland Tribune* during 1931 and 1932. She passed away April 25, 1965.

(Courtesy Jeanne Cason Laing)

Sadie and Wyatt rest together at the Hills of Eternity
Memorial Park Cemetery, Colma, California.

(Courtesy findagrave.com)

NOTES & SOURCES

1. Tefertiller, Casey, *Wyatt Earp: The Life Behind the Legend* (New York, John Wiley & Sons, Inc. 1997) pp 329-335.

2. Ibid.

3. Jay, Roger, *"Face to Face: Sadie Mansfield /Josephine Sarah Marcus"* Wild West History Association (WWHA*) Journal,* Volume VI, No.1 February 2013 pp. 51; Earl Chafin was not an author, but rather an editor who published several manuscripts in the 1990s.

4. Mitchell, Carol, "Lady Sadie" *True West* magazine, February-March 2001.

5. Jay, *Face to Face*, pp. 37-55.

6. Monahan, Sherry, *Mrs. Earp: The Wives and Lovers of the Earp Brothers*; (Guilford, Connecticut, Two Dot, 2013) pp. 58.

7. Monahan, *Mrs. Earp*, pp. 40.

8. Monahan, *Mrs. Earp*, pp. 35.; 1870 federal census of San Francisco, ancestry.com; Josephine's birth certificate has never been found, so her age is based on the census information given in the 1870 and 1880 federal census.

9. 1870 federal census of San Francisco, ancestry.com Aaron was incorrectly listed as "Edward Wener" (sic).

10. Ibid.; *The Elevator* (San Francisco) May 21, 1869; 1869 San Francisco City Directory.

11. Monahan, *Mrs. Earp*, pp. 38.

12. Chafin, Earl (Editor) *Wyatt's Woman: She Married Wyatt Earp, The Life and Times of Josephine Sarah Marcus*; (Riverside, CA, Earl Chafin Press 1996) pp. 5-6.

13. *San Francisco Bulletin*, October 19, 1870. It should be noted that no records for a boy named "Marcus Nathan," of the appropriate age, have been located in the available California census records, or other newspapers of the day. The *San Francisco Morning Call* October 19, 1870, noted that the boy was very small in stature and this fits with the description of Nathan Marcus, who was only five foot seven inches tall, at age 39.

14. *San Francisco Chronicle*, October 27, 1871. It should be noted that the only boy named "Nathan Marcus" of the appropriate age in the San Francisco census records was Josephine's brother.

15. Jay, *Face to Face*, pp 48.

16. 1871 San Francisco City Directory; ancestry.com

17. Jay. *Face to Face* pp 52.; 1873 & 1874 San Francisco City Directory; ancestry.com

18. Chafin *Wyatt's Woman* pp 6. [Edna was actually the name of Sadie's niece.]

19. Chafin *Wyatt's Woman*, pp 7; Brand, Peter; *Doc Holliday's Nemesis: The Story of Johnny Tyler &*

Tombstone's Gamblers' War. (Meadowbank, Australia; Brand Publishing, 2018) pp. 51.

20. 1873 San Francisco City Directory; ancestry.com

21. 1873, 1874 & 1875 San Francisco City Directory; ancestry.com

22. Jay, *Face to Face*, pp. 53.

23. Brand, *Johnny Tyler*, pp. 32-35.

24. 1870 federal census for San Francisco, (Waverly Place); ancestry.com

25. *San Francisco Chronicle*, July 14, 1873.

26. *San Francisco Chronicle*, March 1, 1872; March 16, 1872.

27. *San Francisco Chronicle*, July 14, 1873; July 16, 1873; *San Francisco Morning Call* September 9, 1873.

28. Ibid.; 1870 federal census of San Francisco, ancestry.com; 1873 & 1874 San Francisco City Directory, ancestry.com; Everett Street did not survive the 1906 earthquake and is no longer listed as a street in San Francisco. The timing of the girls' grooming may have coincided with summer school holidays.

29. *San Francisco Morning Call* September 9, 1873; *San Francisco Chronicle,* September 9, 1873.

30. Ibid.

31. Ibid.; *San Francisco Chronicle*, September 12, 1873.

32. *San Francisco Chronicle,* September 9, 1873.

33. *San Francisco Morning Call* September 9, 1873.

34. Ibid.

35. Ibid

36. Winegarner, Beth, *The Hidden, Painful History of San Francisco's Magdalen Asylum*, missionlocal.org, July 1, 2022; *San Francisco Chronicle*, September 9, 1873.

37. *San Francisco Chronicle*, September 10, 1873; *San Francisco Bulletin*, September 10, 1873. For information on "Nellie Schwartz," see mention of her association with Emma Hopper in the *San Francisco Chronicle*, July 16, 1873, and her attempted suicide in the *San Francisco Daily Evening Post*, February 3, 1876.

38. *San Francisco Morning Call*, September 9, 1873.

39. *San Francisco Chronicle*, September 10, 1873.

40. 1880 federal census – Magdalen Asylum inmates; ancestry.com; *The Evening Mail* (Stockton, CA), February 16, 1895; February 20, 1895.

41. *San Francisco Bulletin*, March 19, 1875; *San Francisco Bulletin*, February 23 1877; *San Francisco Examiner,* June 15, 1877.

42. *San Francisco Bulletin*, October 8, 1880; *San Francisco Examiner,* October 9, 1880.

43. *San Francisco Examiner,* October 16, 1880; August 24, 1881; August 31, 1881; October 13, 1881; January 5, 1882.

44. 1874 San Francisco City Directory, ancestry.com; the July, 1873 San Francisco Voter Register confirms

that a butcher named Martin Joseph Fenton was also residing at 221 Clara Street. This address was confirmed when Fenton's wife, Maria, passed away July 3, 1873 after giving birth to a son. Her funeral was conducted from 221 Clara Street – see the *San Francisco Bulletin*, July 1, 1873 & *San Francisco Chronicle*, July 4, 1873. Fenton was no longer living there in 1874, as he was listed as a butcher aboard the *P.M.S.S. Alaska* in the 1874 San Francisco City Directory; *Evening Bulletin,* (San Francisco) December 16, 1873.

45. *San Francisco Morning Call,* March 26, 1874, March 27, 1874; James Dowling, an Irish laborer, and James Dwyer, an Irish newspaper delivery-man were also listed as residing at 221 Clara Street in the 1874 San Francisco City Directory. Dowling was listed in the 1880 federal census as married, without children, and still residing at 221 Clara, while James Dwyer, a single man, moved to 59 Shipley Street by 1875.

46. See the *San Francisco Chronicle*, July 14, 1873 for details of how girls were procured and, other situations the police discovered.

47. Jay, *Face to Face*, pp. 49.

48. 1860 federal census for San Francisco, ancestry.com

49. *Daily Alta* (San Francisco) December 2, 1860; June 2, 1861.

50. U.S. IRS Tax Assessment Lists, 1862-1918; ancestry.com

51. *San Francisco Evening Bulletin*, August 13, 1868; *New York Evening Post,* September 5, 1868.

52. *New York Evening Post,* October 1, 1868; *Sacramento Daily Union*, October 5, 1868; Lizzie Devoe did not make the return trip with Hattie Wells, and must have lingered in New York. Devoe did eventually return to San Francisco and died of liver disease, in a brothel on Dupont Street, on October 3, 1872; California Death Records. ancestry.com

53. *Sacramento Daily Union*, October 26, 1868; *Marysville Daily Appeal* (California), October 29, 1868.

54. *San Francisco Chronicle*, December 19, 1869.

55. Ibid; 1870 federal census for San Francisco; *San Francisco Chronicle,* January 22, 1888.

56. *San Francisco Bulletin*, April 16, 1869; April 20, 1869.

57. *San Francisco Chronicle*, November 14, 1869; November 17, 1869.

58. *San Francisco Chronicle*, October 5, 1870; October 8, 1870.

59. 1870 federal census for San Francisco; It is possible that "Hattie Seymour" was actually "Emma Seymour," who had come from New York City with Wells in October, 1868, as prostitutes often used variations of their names, and more than one alias.

60. *San Francisco Chronicle*, September 13, 1871; December 2, 1872. *Arizona Weekly Miner,* (Prescott) November 2, 1877. An "Ella Howard" was arrested in Chicago in 1865 and 1866 for keeping a brothel, and an "Ella Howard" sailed for San Francisco from New York on the steamship *"Guiding Star"* in June, 1868.

61. New York Arriving Passenger & Crew Lists 1820-1957. ancestry.com

62. *Daily Alta*, (San Francisco) February 23, 1873; Hattie Wells' decision to move out of San Francisco may have related to a change in her family circumstances. Evidence suggests that Wells either gave birth to a baby girl in 1872, or chose to adopt the baby of one of her working girls. The same evidence indicates she named the child after herself – "Hattie Wells." The Prescott *Weekly Miner,* dated November 15, 1878 stated that "little Hattie Wells," a popular child, had fallen and broken her arm. She bravely endured much pain and was attended by the best physician in Prescott. The 1880 federal census for Prescott Arizona, taken on June 15, indicated that Wells had changed her name to "Harriet A. Queen." She was still residing in the same home on Granite Street, in Prescott, and gave her age as 43 [actually 48], born in New York, and widowed. She listed her 8-year-old daughter, now named "Hattie Queen," as being born in California. Wells/Queen employed a Chinese servant, while two houses of prostitution

operated beside her home. Why Wells changed her name to "Queen" is not yet known. Another interesting inclusion in their household was a 22-year-old son, named "William C. Queen," also born in New York. He was listed as a mining engineer.

63. *San Franciso Chronicle*, March 7, 8 & 9, 1873.

64. Victoria F. Behan vs. John H. Behan; divorce filed May 22, 1875 in the District Court, Prescott, Arizona Territory; Arizona State Library and Archive. [hereafter listed as Behan vs. Behan.]

65. 1874 Arizona Territorial Census; Yavapai County; ancestry.com

66. 1874 Arizona Territorial Census; Yavapai County; ancestry.com; *Arizona Weekly Miner*, (Prescott) May 15, 1874; May 22, 1874.

67. *Arizona Weekly Miner* (Prescott) September 18, 1874; *Los Angeles Herald*, September 20, 1874; *Los Angeles Evening Express*, October 5, 1874; *Los Angeles Daily Herald*, October 6, 1874.

68. *San Francisco Examiner*, October 26, 1874, comments on the bad weather at that time.

69. *The Arizona Citizen,* (Tucson) November 8, 1879; *Arizona Daily Star* (Tucson), December 17, 1879; See the 1879 San Francisco City Directory for details of Mary "May" Bell, Actress, at 161 16th Street; Chafin, *Wyatt's Woman*. pp. 12; *San Louis Obispo Weekly Tribune,* November 7, 1874 seems to list the arriving passengers for the previous two weeks, with Howard

and Mansfield at the top of the list. The previous weekly edition had listed no arrivals, which was an obvious omission.

70. *Santa Barbara Daily Press*, November 2, 1874; *Los Angeles Daily Star*, November 6, 1874.

71. *The Elevator* (San Francisco) October 31, 1874.

72. 1860 federal census, Ward 2, Sacramento, CA.

73. 1852 California census; *Sacramento Daily Union,* February 25, 1858.

74. 1860 federal census, Sutter Township, CA.

75. 1860 federal census, Ward 2, Sacramento, CA.

76. *Sacramento Bee*, October 16, 1861; 1866 & 1868 Sacramento City Directory.

77. Sacramento Voter Register, May 10, 1870.

78. 1870 federal census, Ward 2, Sacramento, CA; 1870 Sacramento City Directory.

79. *Sacramento Bee*, September 13, 1871.

80. 1876 Arizona Territorial Census; Yavapai County; ancestry.com; *Arizona Weekly Miner*, (Prescott) December 19, 1881.

81. Chafin, *Wyatt's Woman*, pp. 12; It curious that in the original memoir, the word "negress" was emphasized and typed in capital letters, as NEGRESS, almost begging for the reader's attention. Josephine further stated that "Aunt Julia" was "kind-faced" and "wore a beautiful paisley shawl;" *San Francisco Chronicle*, January 22, 1888 mentions "Aunt Bess."

82. *Tucson Weekly Star*, (AZ) October 23, 1879.

83. *The Arizona Sentinel* (Yuma) October 25, 1879; *Tucson Citizen* (AZ) October 23, 1879; *Tucson Weekly Star,* (AZ) October 23, 1879.

84. Chafin, *Wyatt's Woman.* pp 189.

85. *Arizona Weekly Miner* (Prescott) November 20, 1874.

86. Chafin *Wyatt's Woman.* pp. 192-193; *Arizona Weekly Miner* (Prescott) November 13, 1874.

87. Behan vs. Behan.

88. Ibid.; Chafin, *Wyatt's Woman.* pp. 195.

89. *Arizona Weekly Miner* (Prescott) January 15, 1875; February 5, 1875; Territory of Arizona vs. Sadie Mansfield – Petty Larceny; Arizona State Library and Archive.

90. *Arizona Weekly Miner* (Prescott) April 9, 1875.

91. Behan vs. Behan.

92. 1875 San Francisco City Directory, ancestry.com; *Daily Alta* (San Francisco), July 12, 1875; According to the 1875 San Francisco City Directory, David Arent, a blacksmith, occupied a rear room at 10 Zoe Street, and a laborer, named Timothy Murphy, was also listed at the same address in that same year.

93. *Los Angeles Herald,* November 2, 1875.

94. Chafin, *Wyatt's Woman*, pp. 195-196.

95. 1876 Arizona Territorial Census; Yavapai County; ancestry.com

96. *Los Angeles Evening Express*, February 7, 1876; *Los Angeles Daily Star*, February 8, 1876; *Santa*

Barbara Morning Press, February 12, 1876; *Daily Alta,* (San Francisco) February 14, 1876.

97. Chafin *Wyatt's Woman.* pp. 7; *San Francisco Chronicle,* March 20, 1876.

98. San Francisco City Directory, 1876, ancestry.com

99. *Santa Barbara Morning Press,* May 4, 1876; August 8, 1876; August 9, 1876; *Los Angeles Evening Express,* January 25, 1877.

100. Chafin *Wyatt's Woman,* pp. 197; Jay, *Face to Face,* pp. 50; Sadie had carelessly incriminated herself, yet again, by stating that her runaway, and her illness, had occurred when she was still a schoolgirl.

101. 1877 San Francisco City Directory, ancestry.com; Philip Cramer, a cabinetmaker, was also listed at 10 Zoe Street in 1877; the same address was advertised for rent at $6 per week in 1886, and for $7.50 per week in 1888.

102. 1878 & 1879 San Francisco City Directory, ancestry.com; *Arizona Weekly Miner* (Prescott) May 2, 1879; May 23, 1879; Chafin *Wyatt's Woman.* pp.197. In 1940, Sadie claimed a 3rd Grade education.

103. Chafin, *Wyatt's Woman,* pp. 198.

104. *Phoenix Herald,* February 13, 1880; February 20, 1880; *Arizona Weekly Miner,* (Prescott) March 5, 1880; March 26, 1880; 1880 federal census of Prescott, Arizona.

105. 1880 federal census, conducted 2nd & 3rd June, Tip Top AZ. Interestingly, the census states that Behan

had been unemployed for four months of the year. In the 1910, 1920 & 1930 federal census, Sadie Earp claimed her parents were born in Germany.

106. *San Francisco Bulletin*, April 13, 1880; 1880 San Francisco City Directory; ancestry.com

107. 1880 federal census, San Francisco; ancestry.com; Monahan, *Mrs. Earp*, pp. 49; Chafin, *Wyatt's Woman* pp. 196. A perfect example of a family listing their child at home, even though he was an inmate at the Ohio Reform School for Boys, was Perry Mallon. The 1870 census shows Perry as living at home, but he was also listed correctly as an inmate.

108. *Daily Epitaph* (Tombstone, AZ) September 15, 1880; April 17, 1881; July 29, 1881; Jay, *Face to Face* pp. 47.; *Daily Alta* (San Francisco, CA) August 1, 1881.

109. *Daily Epitaph* (Tombstone, AZ), August 13, 1881; *San Francisco Examiner,* November 21, 1881. The *Daily Epitaph* (Tombstone, AZ), dated November 11, 1881 also stated that "S. Mansfield," of San Francisco, had passed Newhall, CA, heading for Arizona the previous day, perhaps indicating another of Sadie's trips.

110. *Los Angeles Times*, February 24, 1882; *Los Angeles Herald*, February 24, 1882; *Arizona Star* (Tucson), February 25, 1882; *The Tombstone Epitaph,* February 26, 1882;

111. Jay, *Face to Face,* pp. 54.

112. *The Tombstone Epitaph,* April 8, 1882; Arizona Territorial Census, July 1882; ancestry.com

113. *San Francisco Bulletin,* May 29, 1882.

114. *Los Angeles Herald,* July 18, 1882.

115. 1883 San Francisco City Directory.

116. *San Francisco Chronicle,* March 6, 1883.

117. *San Francisco Chronicle*, August 2, 1882.

118. *San Francisco Chronicle,* October 20, 1882; *Sacramento Bee,* October 20, 1882.

119. *Los Angeles Herald*, November 1, 1882.

120. *Seattle Daily Post*, October 31, 1882; Clara Smart had also been listed as an 18-year-old prostitute in Pima County, Arizona in the 1880 federal census.

121. Arizona Territorial Census, July 1882. ancestry.com; *San Francisco Chronicle,* January 22, 1883 showed unclaimed mail for both Virgil and James Earp, and unclaimed mail for James' wife, Bessie, on February, 26, 1883.

122. *San Francisco Chronicle,* March 11, 1883; *San Francisco Bulletin,* March 12, 1883; *San Francisco Chronicle*, April 22, 1883 reported that "the three gamblers arrested in the faro game of William Earp at 3 Morton Street each forfeited $40 bail."

123. *San Francisco Examiner*, March 18, 1883; *Los Angeles Times*, April 10, 1883.

124. *Sacramento Daily Record-Union,* April 6, 1883.

125. *Salt Lake Herald Republican*, (Salt Lake City, Utah) April 7, 1883.

126. *The Solid Muldoon* (Ouray, Colorado), April 20, 1883.

127. Chafin, *Wyatt's Woman*. Chapter 13.

128. Chafin, *Wyatt's Woman*. Chapter 7.

129. Ibid.

130. *Garden City Irrigator* (Kansas), June, 14, 1883; *The Daily Commonwealth* (Topeka, Kansas), June 15, 1883.

131. 1882, 1883, 1885, 1886 & 1887 San Francisco City Directories; *San Francisco Examiner*, July 7, 1883. The records show that Emil Lehnhardt and his wife, Henrietta, continued to reside in San Francisco from 1883 to 1887. They did not move to Oakland until later in 1887. The Oakland City Directories and the Oakland Voter Registers, show they lived at 1115 West Street, Oakland from 1890 to 1896, and at 1120 West Street, Oakland from 1898 to 1904. They moved into a newly built home on Telegraph Ave. in 1904.

132. *Salt Lake Herald-Republican* (Salt Lake City, Utah) August 30, 1883; September 21, 1883.

133. *The Galveston Daily News* (Texas), December 1, 1883; December 23, 1883.

134. Chafin, *Wyatt's Woman*. pp. 197.

135. Chafin, *Wyatt's Woman*, pp. 196, 194

136. Chafin, *Wyatt's Woman*, pp 196. Sadie's use of the words "humiliation and regret," were far too strong and emotive to relate to the fairytale she told in her memoir. The wording hinted of far darker pursuits.

INDEX

Ackerman, Vinnolia Earp, 6, 7, 20, 126

Adams, Florence, 42, 47, 53, 53

Alice, Minnie, 60, 66

Andrews, Germima "Jennie," 53, 69

Arent, David, 136

Arnold, Kate, 42

Asher's store (Prescott), 69

Baldwin, Elias "Lucky," 110

Beatty, Willie, 73

Behan, Albert, 79, 85

Behan, John Harris, 52, 53, 67-69, 71, 75, 79-83, 85, 86

Behan, Josephine (see also Marcus, Josephine; Mansfield, Sadie; Earp, Josephine "Sadie"), 85, 86

Behan, Victoria, 53, 71

Belasco family, 19, 24

Bell, Mary "May," 57-59, 65, 136

Bell, Minnie, 42, 44

Benjamin, Carrie, 12

Bess, "Aunt", 44, 64

Blaylock, Celia Ann "Mattie" (see also Earp, "Mattie" 5, 88, 89, 94, 98

Blaylock, Elizabeth "Betsy," 95
Bowers, Ed, 69
Brooke, Gideon, 83
Burton, Claiborne (see also Hubbard, Claiborne), 61-63
Burton, Julia "Aunt" (see also Hubbard, Julia "Aunt"), 60-66, 83, 137

Cain, Andrew, 35
Cain, Thomas, 35
Carpenter, Harry, 65
Cason, Mabel Earp, 6, 7, 20, 106, 127
Casselli, Tom, 65
Cassidy, Bridget, 24, 25, 27, 29, 30
Cassidy, Catherine "Katy," 24-26, 29, 30, 34, 35, 38, 107
Cassidy, John, 24, 25
Cassidy, Mary, 24, 34, 35, 38
Chafin, Earl, 7
Clark, Mollie (aka Molly), 46, 47
Clements, Julia, 47
Coffey, John, 28
Courtney, Brad, 3, 68

Dauphin, Joe, 65
Davis "Jeff," 73, 74
Devitt, Edward, 28
Devoe, Lizzie, 41, 134

Dowling, James, 133
Dunning, Lizzie, 53
Duval, Maud, 42, 44
Dwyer, James, 131

Earp, Allie, 90, 92, 98
Earp, Bessie, 90, 141
Earp, James, 90, 95, 98, 141
Earp, Josephine "Sadie" (see also Marcus, Josephine
    "Sadie;" Behan, Josephine; Mansfield, Sadie),
    5-10, 96, 101, 108-113, 116, 122, 125-128
Earp, "Mattie" (see also Blaylock, Celia A. "Mattie"),
88, 90, 94, 95, 98
Earp, Morgan, 89, 90
Earp, Virgil, 90-93, 96, 98, 141
Earp, Warren Baxter, 89, 90, 92-94, 96, 98
Earp, Wyatt S. (see also Stapp, W. B.), 5-7, 87, 89, 90,
92-94, 98-105, 109-112, 114-116, 118, 121, 123, 128

Fromberg family, 19, 24

Gardner, Mary, 53
Green, Johnny "Crooked Mouth," 104, 105

Haynes, Gertrude (see also Pring, Gertrude), 65
Hewitt, Belle (see also Howitt, Belle), 57, 65
Hirsch, Dora (see also Hirschberg, Leah), 17, 24, 39,
57

Hirsch, Mrs. (see also Hirschberg, Betsy), 17

Hirschberg, Betsy (see also Hirsch, Mrs.), 17

Hirschberg, Leah (see also Hirsch, Dora), 17, 24, 39

Hirschberg, Meyer, 17

Holliday, John Henry "Doc," 91

Hopper, Emma, 25, 26, 33, 132

Howard, Ella, 39, 47, 48, 52, 53, 59, 66, 70, 71, 135

Howitt, Belle (aka Hewitt, Belle), 57-59, 65

Hubbard, Claiborne (see also Burton, Claiborne), 61-63

Hubbard, Julia "Aunt" (see also Burton, Julia "Aunt"), 60-65, 137

Jay, Roger, 3, 7, 9, 10, 17, 39, 56

Jordan, Millie, 53

Laing, Jeanne Cason, 126, 127

Lake, Stuart, 5, 101, 111, 123

Lamont, Eva, 47

Lawrence, Willis, 91

Lee, Minna "Minnie," 47

Lehnhardt, Edna, 125, 130

Lehnhardt, Emil, 102, 117-120, 125, 142

Lehnhardt, Emil Jnr., 119

Lehnhardt, Henrietta "Hattie" (see also Marcus, Henrietta "Hattie"), 6, 112, 118, 119, 124, 125, 142

Levy, Rebecca (see also Marcus, Rebecca; Wiener, Rebecca), 11
Lewis, Jeffreys, 108
Lewis, Sophia (see also Marcus, Sophia), 11
Louderback, Davis, 30, 32, 33, 46

Mallon, Perry, 140
Mansfield, Josie, 56
Mansfield, Sadie (alias of Marcus, Josephine "Sadie" aka Marks, Josephine), 7, 55, 56, 59, 60, 63, 66, 67, 69-77, 82, 83, 86, 87, 89, 90, 93, 94, 96, 113
Marcus, Henrietta "Hattie" (see also Lehnhardt, Henrietta "Hattie"), 11, 12, 16, 17, 37, 84
Marcus, Hyman "Henry", 11, 12, 15, 33, 38, 84
    (also known as)
    Marcon, Henry, 76
    Marcusa, Henry, 79
    Marcuse, Henry, 16, 72, 79
    Marcuse, Hyman, 15
    Marks, Henry, 19, 36
    Maroux, Henry, 12
Marcus, Josephine "Sadie" (see also Marks, Josephine; Earp, Josephine "Sadie"; Mansfield, Sadie), 11-20, 35, 55, 81, 84,
Marcus, Nathan (see also Marks, Nathan; Markus, Nathan; Nathan, Marcus), 11, 13-15, 79, 84, 85, 130

Marcus, Rebecca (see also Levy, Rebecca; Wiener, Rebecca), 11

Marcus, Sophia (see also Lewis, Sophia), 11, 15, 27, 33, 38, 79, 84, 85, 88, 113

Markham, Pauline, 2, 57, 64, 65, 72, 83, 106

Marks, Jake, 72, 73

Marks, Josephine (see also Marcus, Josephine), 24-39

Marks, Nathan (see also Marcus, Nathan; Markus, Nathan; Nathan, Marcus), 36, 72

Markus, Nathan (see also Marks, Nathan; Marcus, Nathan), 36

Marquis, Sarah, 95

Martin, John, 35

Masterson, "Bat," 102, 108

McCarthy, Dave, 46

McCarty brothers & sisters (Dance School), 16, 17

McCloud, Anna, 27

McCloud, Annie, 24-26, 29, 38

McCloud, Elizabeth "Lizzie," 24-26, 29, 30, 34, 38, 107

McMahon, Randolph, 65

Mihaljevich, Mike, 3, 20, 75

Mitchell, Carol, 3, 7, 9, 10, 56

Monahan, Sherry, 3, 9, 10, 84

Moore, Mrs., 27

Morgan, Susan, 40, 41

Nathan, Marcus (see also Marcus, Nathan; Markus, Nathan; Marks, Nathan), 13, 14

Pennington, Mollie, 42
Powers, Minnie, 71, 76, 77
Pring, Gertrude (see also Haynes, Gertrude), 65

Queen, Harriet A., (see also Wells, Hattie A.) 135, 136
Queen, Hattie Jnr., (see also Wells, Hattie Jnr.) 135
Queen, William C., 136

Reese, Nancy "Nellie", 26, 28, 30, 33
Rewitsky, "Dutch Charley" (alias Watkins), 45, 46
Rickabaugh, Lew, 110
Roraback, Frank, 65

Schwartz, Nellie, 33, 132
Seymour, Emma, 42, 45, 46, 134
Seymour, Hattie, 47, 134
Short, Luke, 100, 101
Smart, Clara, 95, 141
Smart, May, 95,
Spader, William, 12
Stapp, W. B. (alias of Wyatt S. Earp), 93
Stevens, Ameila, 53

Wakely, Rosa, 53
Watkins (alias Rewitsky, "Dutch Charley"), 45

Wells, Hattie A., (see also Queen, Harriet A.) 39-54, 56, 60, 63, 64, 66, 80, 135, 136

Wells, Hattie Jnr., (see also Queen, Hattie Jnr,) 135

Wiener, Aaron, 11, 72, 79, 83, 84, 125, 129

Wiener, Isaac, 11, 72

Wiener, Rebecca (see also Levy, Rebecca; Marcus, Rebecca), 11, 17, 18, 55, 113, 125

Other books by Peter Brand,
available world-wide at Amazon.com

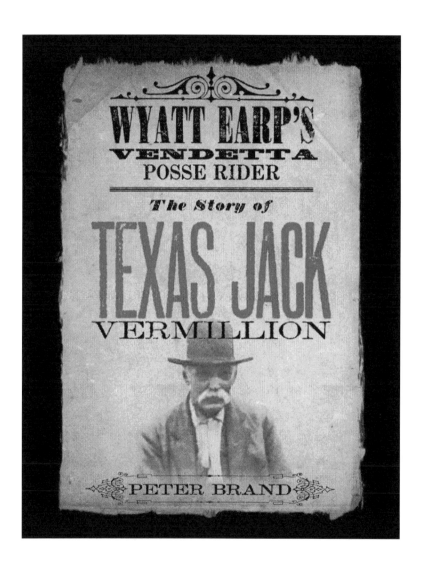

Other books by Peter Brand,
available world-wide at Amazon.com

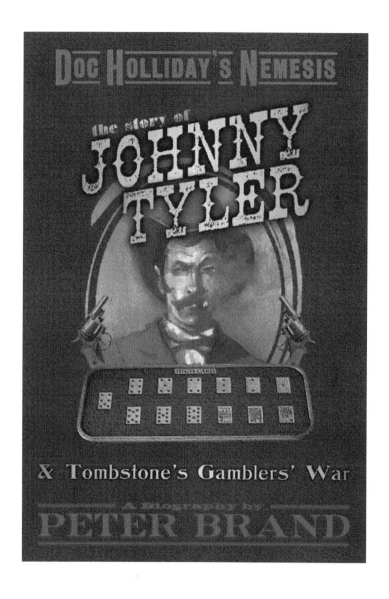

Other books by Peter Brand,
available world-wide at Amazon.com

Made in United States
Troutdale, OR
01/09/2025

27780953R10093